Soviet Satire of the Twenties

University of Florida Monographs

Humanities Number 47

Soviet Satire of the Twenties

Richard L. Chapple

A University of Florida Book

University Presses of Florida
FAMU/FAU/FIU/FSU/UCF/UF/UNF/USF/UWF
Gainesville

University Presses of Florida is the central agency for scholarly publishing of the State of Florida's university system. Its offices are located at 15 NW 15th Street, Gainesville, FL 32603. Works published by University Presses of Florida are evaluated and selected for publication by a faculty editorial committee of any one of Florida's nine public universities: Florida A&M University (Tallahassee), Florida Atlantic University (Boca Raton), Florida International University (Miami), Florida State University (Tallahassee), University of Central Florida (Orlando), University of Florida (Gainesville), University of North Florida (Jacksonville), University of South Florida (Tampa), University of West Florida (Pensacola).

Library of Congress Cataloging in Publication Data

Chapple, Richard L.   1944–
  Soviet satire of the twenties.

  (University of Florida monographs: Humanities; no. 47)
  "A University of Florida book."
  Bibliography: p.
  Includes index
  1. Russian literature—20th century—History and criticism.   2. Satire, Russian—History and criticism.
I. Title.   II. Series: Florida. University, Gainesville. University of Florida monographs: Humanities; no. 47.
PG3026.S3C47   1980   891.7'7'4209   79–23575
ISBN 0–8130–0643–0

Preface

THIS BOOK is an attempt to categorize the factors that produced Soviet satire and to analyze their development from October 1917 through the imposition of Socialist Realism as the prescribed technique of literature and literary criticism. The focus is on the initiation and development of themes and stereotypes and on the contributions made by individual satirists. Lengthy critical evaluation of individual works is sacrificed to a generalized picture of satire's flourishing and demise. The book is intended for those who have only a superficial knowledge of satire or Soviet literature, as well as dedicated students of things Russian. For this reason all quoted passages are translated. Thus, the book can make certain lesser-known facts of Soviet literature available to a larger audience, who will then be interested in further pursuit of knowledge and understanding in this area.

The transliteration of Russian into English follows System I as found in J. Thomas Shaw, *The Transliteration of Modern Russian for English-Language Publications* (Madison: University of Wisconsin Press, 1967). Some concessions have been made for the sake of accepted English spelling (for example, Ehrenburg and Meyerhold rather than Erenburg and Meyerkhold) or to attain a more logical rendering (for example: Alexander for Alexandr, Vicar Dooley for Vikary Dyuli, Goose for Gus, von Rebenkov for fon Rebenkov, Pierre for Per, Kemble for Kembl, Hayes for Kheys, Julio for Khulio, Tvaift for Tvayvt, Delais for Dele, Schmidt for Shmidt, Jebbs for Dzhebs, Williams Hardyle for Viliams Khardayl, Mr. Cool for Mr. Kul, Don Ruy for Don Ryuy, Wrangel for Vrangel, and Renaissance for Renesans).

Titles of works are both transliterated and translated the first time they appear; thereafter the translation is used. The only exceptions are works which are titled with a person's name, for example, *M. P. Sinyagin* or "Gompers." These titles appear alone without the duplicate translation. All footnotes and bibliographical items are both transliterated and translated. This format will facilitate the book's use by readers with no background in Russian.

Unless otherwise noted all translations are my own. Many thanks go to Prof. John J. Bobkoff for his helpful suggestions in rendering heretofore untranslated titles and passages.

Additional thanks go to the Graduate School of the University of Florida for making possible the publication of this monograph.

Acknowledgments

THE AUTHOR wishes to thank the following publishers for permission to quote from their books:

Paul Elek Ltd., London: Ilya Ehrenburg, *The Stormy Life of Laz Roitshvantz*, translated by Alec Brown (1965).

Oxford University Press, London: M. V. Glenny, "Mikhail Bulgakov," *Survey* 65 (October 1967):9.

Iowa State University Press, Ames: Leonard Feinberg, *The Satirist: His Temperament, Motivation, and Influence* (1960).

University of Oklahoma Press, Norman: Gleb Struve, *Russian Literature under Lenin and Stalin, 1917–1953* (1971).

Pantheon Books, a Division of Random House, Inc., New York: Mikhail Zoshchenko, *Nervous People and Other Satires*, edited by Hugh McLean (1963).

Contents

TO THE MEMORY OF MY FATHER
MAX D. CHAPPLE

1. The Background

THE FLOWERING of Russian satire occurred at a time for which the epithet *Soviet* must be used instead of *Russian*, and at a time of great political chaos, social upheaval, and economic hardship—the decade of the 1920s. The flowering was comparatively belated, inasmuch as satire, long a part of Russian literature, had initially appeared in the form of anonymous popular tales in the sixteenth and seventeenth centuries and had become established with the emergence of Neoclassicism in the eighteenth century. During the second half of the eighteenth century satire was firmly entrenched in the literary world and was making inroads into journalism. The combination of satire and journalism was significant because of its relationship to politics. The politically oriented journalism of the 1770s and 1780s was the first step toward the flourishing of satire in the twenties and provided the historical basis for Soviet satirical *agitprop* (agitation propaganda).

For its influence on satire in the twenties, the nineteenth century is most significant because of the careers of Nikolay Gogol and Mikhail Saltykov-Shchedrin, who are regarded as tsarist Russia's outstanding satirists. Although exact parallels cannot be drawn, these two writers can be considered examples of the two classical trends of satire— Horatian and Juvenalian. The gentle exposé of Horatian satire makes use of laughter and humor and aims to persuade the reader in a bemused fashion. Juvenalian satire, in contrast, is an angry and sometimes violent form of satire that is punitive and that verges on invective and sarcasm. A rhetorical and declamatory style is common for Juvenalian satire, which frequently is intended to destroy its object. Neither type exists in pure form in Russian literature, but Horatian satire became the most prevalent principally due to the far-reaching influence of Gogol.

Toward the end of the nineteenth century, satire significantly declined as literature was dominated first by Populism and then by

Modernism. Neither of these literary trends made extensive use of satire; the elevated problems of religion and the human condition occupied most serious writers of the day. Satirical journalism reappeared during the years 1905–7 in newspapers and the so-called thick magazines, prompted principally by the intense political activity at the turn of the century that resulted in feuding among the several political factions and ultimately in the abortive Revolution of 1905. This brief period of rejuvenation was, for all practical discussion, confined to the newspapers and magazines and did not appreciably affect belles-lettres.

To a great extent the satirical mode was inactive between the revolutions as the poetical *-isms* of Modernism (Decadence, Symbolism, Acmeism, and Futurism) dominated literature. The notable exception, the journal *Satirikon,* flourished during the intervening decade largely through the efforts of N. A. Teffi (pseudonym of Nadezhda Buchinskaya), Arkady Averchenko, and Sasha Chyorny (pseudonym of Alexander Glyukberg), all of whom eventually emigrated. It was only after October and two years of civil war that satire truly came into its own; this rebirth in 1919 was again initiated, as the earlier rejuvenation had been, by feuilletons, sketches, and poems in the magazines and newspapers. At this time, however, satire became an integral part of Russian belles-lettres. Also, as important as the massive journalistic activity was, the lasting monuments and greatest creativity were found in the prose and, to a lesser extent, the poetry of the twenties.

Satire was by no means a homogeneous movement during the decade, and three distinct periods may be identified, each with its own characteristics. The periods are essentially those into which Soviet literature of the twenties as a whole is traditionally divided: War Communism, 1917–21; NEP (the New Economic Policy), 1922–27; and the first Five-Year Plan, 1928–32. These periods produced two amorphous camps and four general factions with one or another of which all satirists may be identified.

The large camps were delineated politically and may be termed simply proregime and antiregime, that is, for or against the new Soviet regime. Each camp may be divided further into two factions: agitprop and moderate proregime in the proregime camp, and Fellow Travelers and emigrés in the antiregime camp. These factions reflected a certain amount of ideological divergence, and on some issues the boundaries were vague. For example, moderate proregime satirists and the Fellow Travelers sometimes spoke with essentially the same voice on the same issues. There was often as much diversity in literary technique and aesthetics within the factions of each camp as between the camps themselves. Ultimately it was politics that fashioned the tenuous and informal alliances.

The Fellow Traveler faction harbored two principal groups: the liberal and humanitarian representatives of the intelligentsia whose politics were moderately left wing and who only conditionally accepted the Revolution, and moderate socialists, who accepted the Revolution but who felt aesthetically more comfortable in the more reserved atmosphere surrounding the Fellow Travelers. The common literary foundation for these groups was Modernist poetry and classical Russian realism modified by the innovations of the ornamentalists. The emigrés shared this same literary foundation while exhibiting a more radical political posture, usually conservative monarchism or progressive socialism. They are included with the Fellow Travelers in the antiregime camp because they treated the same themes in essentially the same way; the difference was one of degree rather than substance.

The proregime camp featured radical socialists, whose forte was agitprop; government supporters, who employed modernistic techniques as well as propaganda; proletarians and peasants trying to initiate a new culture; and writers such as Ilya Ehrenburg and Alexey Tolstoy, who belonged to the proregime camp because of expediency and an inherent dislike of certain elements of bourgeois—particularly Western—life. The literary foundation for this camp was essentially that of the Fellow Travelers but modified by peculiarly revolutionary developments. In effect, political adherence to the new government glued these writers together, making it possible to speak of them as a literary camp.

The period of War Communism, largely prefatory to the apex of satire in the mid-twenties, featured a search for genre and technique, the definition of satirical subjects, and the beginning of what was to be the fatal involvement with politics.

Immediately after the Revolution, satire was produced largely in feuilletons, satirical sketches, and short stories in the magazines and newspapers, and until approximately 1921 these publicistic forms predominated. The traditional distinction between belles-lettres and feuilletons is only partially valid for this period. Soviet critic A. N. Starkov distinguishes at least three types of feuilleton: those which retained the mass-medium qualities of a newspaper article; those which were closer to belles-lettres and resembled the sketch or short story, as in the works of Ilya Ilf, Yevgeny Petrov, and Valentin Kataev; and those exhibiting the qualities of a magazine article, that is, differing from its newspaper counterpart primarily in length and in a closer approximation to belles-lettres.[1] Although it was closer to the literary sketch than to the newspaper feuilleton, the magazine type of feuilleton did not yet take on the short-story manner developed by the proregime satirists.

Feuilletons were employed mainly by the proregime camp. The newspaper and magazine feuilletons were used primarily by agitprop satirists concerned with mass dissemination of short works for easy reading. Moderate proregime satirists, most notably Kataev, Ilf, and Petrov, preferred what one may call the literary feuilleton, which was the most significant literary result of this publicistic activity.

In 1921 longer prose works began to appear, and the novel, the *povest* (tale), and the short story became the most popular and successful vehicles of satire during the decade. Among the first to appear were somewhat journalistic novel-feuilletons or novel-pamphlets, many of which were directed against foreign bourgeois elements. The first and most important was Ilya Ehrenburg's *Julio Jurenito*,[2] followed by such propagandistic works as Mikhail Levidov's *Diktatura pustyakov (Angliya v pamflete)* [*Dictatorship of Trifles (England in a Pamphlet)*], written in 1923. Because of the author's bent for reportage *Julio Jurenito* served as a model for those who wrote exposé novels, which were most commonly directed against the West. Ehrenburg himself was just as critical of the problems in the Soviet Union as of those in Western Europe, but those who used *Julio Jurenito* as a prototype were proregime satirists interested in belittling the West. Ehrenburg's cynicism toward certain attitudes and institutions at home and abroad was transformed into an ideological indictment of bourgeois and militaristic Western life by those who used the model. The Juvenalian satire in such works resulted in a plethora of overly didactic, second-rate works, which continue to appear.

Another type of longer work appearing early in the decade was the chronicle-*povest*, which quite probably found its inspiration in Alexander Pushkin's *Istoria Sela Goryukhina (History of the Manor of Goryukhino)* and particularly in Saltykov's *Istoria odnogo goroda (History of a Town)*.[3] Such works, initially little more than accusatory reportage, concentrated on the negative prerevolutionary elements that remained in society. The chronicle format was ideal for the unmasking procedure that dominated this genre, since a "before-and-after" sequence could be shown. Initially neither the novel-pamphlet nor the chronicle-povest contained a great deal of humor, and the novel-pamphlet continued to use a ridiculing tone throughout the decade. The chronicle did make more use of humor during NEP, but it never achieved the saturation of humor that marked the more successful works of the period, particularly the short story and sketch. Successful fusion of humor and the long narrative form into the satirical novel was left for Ilf and Petrov later in the decade, with *Dvenadtsat stuliev* (*The Twelve Chairs*) and *Zolotoy telyonok* (*The Golden Calf*).

Another significant development in this prefatory period was the appearance of the utopian satirical novel in the work of Yevgeny Zamyatin, who not only pioneered the genre in the Soviet period but also wrote the most outstanding example, *My* (*We*). The genre was never fully exploited, although Anatoly Lunacharsky, Sergey Bobrov, Lev Lunts, and Vladimir Mayakovsky, among others, experimented with utopias later during NEP. The reasons for the infrequent use of the genre can only be surmised. Certainly, the furor caused by *We* discouraged the use of some utopian motifs, themes, and philosophies even though literature during the early and middle twenties enjoyed a good deal of freedom. Also the twenties showed a remarkable uniformity of subject matter in that the Revolution and contemporary reality dominated all other themes. By and large the Revolution was treated on its own terms, whether from a romantic, political, or naturalistic point of view, and postrevolutionary socialist utopias did not prove as popular as the chaotic reality of October itself. The voluminous themes of contemporary reality were treated differently in each of the three periods: the life of deprivation during War Communism; speculation, the philistine, and the inconsistencies of Soviet life during NEP; and the mobilization of the country toward the abstract and often poorly defined goal of building a socialist society during the first Five-Year Plan. In all periods the impact of the Revolution on the daily lives of the citizens was treated, and even though life changed, this general concern remained the same.

A fourth movement, which grew out of the Revolution itself and developed during the first period, was agitprop. One must be skeptical of referring to much of what was written under the guise of agitation propaganda as literature, since slogans and posters comprised much of the output and the *Okno satiry* ROSTA (*The Window of Satire* of the Russian Telegraphic Agency) was the primary disseminator of the material. Also, many of the poems produced for many years by

Mayakovsky and by the acknowledged poet laureate of the Revolution and spokesman for Stalin, Demyan Bedny, were little more than rhymed slogans designed to "educate" the masses. The verse feuilleton became a popular genre of agitprop because of its adaptability to newspapers and satirical magazines and because satirists could easily isolate and emphasize slogans. The satire was usually mixed with a significant amount of exposé humor, with internal class enemies as well as foreign politics and political leaders the prime targets.

The principal objects of satire for all the literary movements during War Communism were remnants of the past, the Revolution and the changes it brought, and the Civil War. Fellow Travelers and emigrés concentrated on the horrors of life during the Civil War and the brutality of the Reds, while proregime satirists declaimed the ineptitude, brutality, and aristocratic pretensions of the Whites, the Entente intervention in the Civil War, and the political leaders of the Entente nations.

The satirical archetypes were defined for the most part in this initial period. Most of them were traditional types already in Russian literature, but a few were products of the first decade of Soviet leadership. Politics played the dominant role in both the selection and depiction of archetypes. From the outset, the new regime, operating within a tradition of governmental literary censorship, made it clear that despite the relatively free literary atmosphere there were still some "do's" and "don't's," especially in the realm of depicting satirical figures. Satirical archetypes are one of the fountainheads of satirical portrayal,[4] but it immediately became evident that some were safer to depict than others: "Satire has shown the same pattern of growth as other literary forms: it developed richly in the twenties, then settled into a domestic routine as a handmaiden of the state, directing its barbs at preselected 'bourgeois' or 'imperialist' targets. And even in the twenties the satirist could expose the stupidity of evil fools only at some risk, and usually he chose to avoid prime targets in favor of generalized vices, fantastic rogues, or the ever-present 'philistine.' "[5] The list of safe archetypes included these: the White, the aristocrat, the bureaucrat, foreign imperialists, capitalists, religious figures, the bourgeois remnant of the past, the philistine, the emigré, the kulak, the intellectual, the embezzler, the drunk, the hooligan, and the corrupt petty official. The same generalizations may be made for both institutions and human foibles as satirical targets: the safe institutions were those most intimately linked with the tsarist past, such as the church, or those still functioning in the West, while the admissible vices and foibles were attributes of the past or of citizens of Western Europe and the United States.

The techniques of unmasking the archetype were also drawn from existing Russian satire and developed during this prefatory period. The techniques usually acquired a Soviet coloration, however. One of the most prevalent techniques was the use of unflattering and humor-provoking names, either derived from common words or depending upon a comic phonetic effect: for example, Professor Filipp Filippovich Preobrazhensky in Mikhail Bulgakov's *Sobachie serdtse* (*Heart of a Dog*), whose name is derived from the Russian verb "to transfigure" and who performs a symbolic operation on a dog which changes it into the new Soviet man, and King Sizi-Buzi in Bulgakov's "Bagrovy ostrov" ("The Crimson Island"), who represents Tsar Nikolay II and who is as flippant and scatterbrained as the sound of his name would suggest. In each instance character is exposed semantically.

The archetype was also exposed through his personal life, physical appearance, and personality traits. Physical details were used frequently because they made possible immediate characterization through the use of certain stereotyped distinctive features. White hands, obesity, and "avaricious" eyes quickly identified the White for the Soviet reader. Fellow Travelers and emigrés used snarling mouths, coarse features, and vicious eyes to expose the brutal and unfeeling Communist. Archetypes were seldom without revealing physical attributes that reduced them to something less than human, usually animals or automatons. Through caricature, hyperbole, and burlesque, the reduction of the vital to the mechanical was accomplished. This method was used particularly by Fellow Traveler and emigré satirists to demonstrate the harmful effects of the Revolution and communism on mankind. Arkady Averchenko, Zamyatin, and Mikhail Zoshchenko were the principal practitioners of this type of reduction. Aspects of personal life included the character's interaction with others, in particular his family; his eating habits, which could deteriorate to an animal function (or even to cannibalism) or become a pretentious and ornate ritual; his sex life, often reduced to perversion or shrouded in ineptitude; his clothing, frequently pretentious; and his manner of death—satirical figures usually die in a vainglorious or absurd manner.

Despite the rich descriptive possibilities of characters' personal lives, they were not normally portrayed in great detail. Instead, a few traits were singled out and repeated, often becoming leitmotifs associated with the character, even replacing him at times through such devices as metonymy and personification. In this latter technique of unmasking, the legacy of Gogol is evident. Gogolian technique (hyperbole, intentional illogicality, mixture of styles) is most obvious in authors who were not using satire to promote the Soviet regime. Thus, it was the Fellow Travelers, most notably Bulgakov, who most revealed his influence in their technique. Proregime satirists also looked back to Gogol, but they viewed him through the prism of the Radical Critics and the socially conscious literature of the nineteenth century and, therefore, saw him almost exclusively as a social critic. Gogol and Saltykov were often invoked as the pioneers and authorities in social criticism, and several literary allusions were made to each.

In order to unmask the archetype and his world, some implicit moral or social standard must be evident. Historically the direct moralizer was the most common way of achieving the goal of unmasking. Other methods, however, are artistically more successful and desirable:

> The easiest way of establishing the necessary reference points is to provide a spokesman for the truth. . . . The method of the direct moralizer has been considerably improved upon by those authors of formal satire who distance themselves from their satirists and attempt to support his standards by showing him leading a reasonable life and reflecting in his person the advantages of his approach to existence.
>
> But the most successful methods for showing that the satiric world is askew have developed from more oblique approaches to the problem. The most common of these techniques has been to build into the satiric plot suggestions, images, of more normative and time-tested modes of conduct and systems of value, which are validated once again by showing the disastrous consequences of failing to observe them.[6]

All of these techniques were established during War Communism: positive characters offsetting satirical, negative ones; positive images and modes of conduct; the author's direct comments refuting the satirically depicted world; the direct moralizer or *raisonneur*; and the failure of the negative world or character without an alternative positive character, institution, or author's comment. The more second-rate and propagandistic the work of literature, the more frequent the use of the authorial comment or positive-character monologue to accomplish the unmasking. More artistic and subtle works tended to infuse the plot with the antidote to the poison.

The Soviet satirical character reacts to his unmasking in a variety of ways: he is unmasked and his harmful influence is made known to the reader and other characters, but he remains the same; he is unmasked and realizes that his path is wrong in a moment of recognition, but the author stops the work before any kind of a rebirth or regeneration can occur; or he is unmasked and changes his life. During War Communism the character was exposed but seldom changed. As the decade progressed, proregime satirists emphasized the rebirth of the character due to the therapeutic force of communism.

A traditional corollary to the technique of unmasking and reaction is the special case of the satirically depicted negative world, which the author allows to continue unpunished. The best examples in the nineteenth century were the parts of Alexander Sukhovo-Kobylin's dramatic trilogy called "Delo" ("The Affair") and "Smert Tarelkina" ("The Death of Tarelkin"), in which the grotesque world of Antichrist triumphs. In the Soviet era this sort of authorial "laxity" was taboo. Satirical pictures of the West had to include their demise, while negative elements of Soviet society were to be overcome by communism. Those works of Soviet literature which allowed a satirically depicted non-Soviet character to continue living untouched by the Revolution, or which showed an unchanged and seemingly unchangeable negative world, met with official criticism and sometimes censorship. The best example of this is Bulgakov's *Heart of a Dog*, in which Professor Preobrazhensky continues his prerevolutionary life of luxury despite the efforts of the local housing committee. It is significant that the work was never published during Bulgakov's life.

The ways in which satirists reacted to people and living conditions during War Communism are indicative of the approaches taken throughout the decade. Both the antiregime and proregime camps frequently based their approach on the perception of incongruity. During this initial period incongruity for Fellow Travelers and emigrés lay in the dichotomy of Soviet promises and claims versus war and deprivation. For the proregime satirist, both moderate and agitprop, incongruity was seen as the contrast between the Soviet attempt to build paradise and the subversive efforts of the Whites and interventionists. These opposing views of reality, founded largely on politics, provided the basis for satire in the 1920s. Incongruity during War Communism was a function of October and was expressed, characteristically, in a bitter and mocking tone. Only during NEP did social, economic, and personal factors, presented in a humorous light, temper the portrayal. Zoshchenko's "laughter through tears" during NEP is an outgrowth of the strained humor and bitter laments of the war years.

Fantasy was extensively employed to create another world in which to reveal the incongruity the author saw in the known world. This fantasy world might be separated dramatically in time and space as in Zamyatin's *We* or Tolstoy's *Giperboloyd Inzhenera Garina* (*Engineer Garin's Hyperboloid*) or *Aelita*; it could be easily accessible through travel, as in Valentin Kataev's *Rastratchiki* (*The Embezzlers*) or Ilf and Petrov's *The Golden Calf* and *The Twelve Chairs*; or it could be limited to the imagination of an individual, as in Yury Olesha's *Zavist* (*Envy*). Allegory suffused such fantasy worlds, which usually represented the modern Soviet state. The Soviet government was portrayed either positively as in *Aelita* or negatively as in *We*; there was little middle ground.

The fate of humor in the Juvenalian satire of War Communism is indicative of its role throughout the decade. Generally, the antiregime camp used more humor than the proregime camp but only during NEP and the first Five-Year Plan. During the Civil War humor slumped first to mockery and then to invective. Laughing at someone has always been a way to expose him; but almost immediately after the Revolution it was evident that the Fellow Travelers and emigrés wanted to disparage October and the Communist, and the proregime writers were more intent on punishing than at laughing at internal class enemies, Western capitalists, and imperialists. Can humor, when it becomes sufficiently personal and splenetic to be invective, still be satire? The trend toward invective is evident in agitprop, and it seems best to call much of it simply propaganda rather than satire or even literature.

During War Communism the term *Soviet* was already becoming ambiguous. Certainly, those involved in agitprop and those writing from the proregime point of view could be said to be writing Soviet satire. Yet while these two groups comprised the majority of those writing, the superior literature was written by the Fellow Travelers. Fellow Traveler satire can be termed Soviet only because it was written after October and dealt largely with contemporary Soviet reality, inasmuch as the point of view and intent were quite different from that expressed in the works of the proregime camp. A further complication is the large number of writers who emigrated and continued nonrevolutionary trends of Russian literature abroad. This group was even less kindly disposed to October and the changes it wrought than were the Fellow Travelers, and even abroad their satiric barbs concentrated largely on contemporary Soviet reality rather than on life in emigration or on the inhabitants and institutions of their new lands. Thus, the treatment of essentially the same material by all of these groups, admittedly with differences in emphasis and concentration, justifies their being discussed together as writers of Soviet satire.

The fact that satire arose once more during War Communism supports Leonard Feinberg's generalization that "the theory that the ideal environment for satire is a changing, unstable society is logical and persuasive."[7] Satirists found ample material in the turbulence of the Civil War years among remnants of the past and indications of the imperfect nature of the present and future. The influence of censorship has already been touched upon with reference to those topics that it was safe to satirize both during and after War Communism. The practical effect of the "do's" and "don't's," however, is problematical: "Kenneth Burke sums up this paradoxical aspect of satire's relation with the law by suggesting that 'the conditions are "more favorable" to satire under censorship than under liberalism—for the most inventive satire arises when the artist is seeking simultaneously to take risks and escape punishment for his boldness, and is never quite certain himself whether he will be acclaimed or punished.' "[8] Or, as Feinberg says, "What it finally comes down to is that censorship determines not whether satire is written but the form of satire that is written, by requiring varying degrees of subterfuge."[9] Censorship succeeded in pitting satirist against satirist and eventually in driving talented men like Zamyatin and Bulgakov either abroad or underground. It did not prevent a good deal of anti-Soviet satire from being written, but the Communist Party itself was unsure of the position it should take, and, while strictures definitely existed, they were not nearly so severe as they were to become in the thirties.

The motivation of the Soviet satirist during War Communism and throughout the decade bears examination and comparison with the traditional and historical factors that prompt the satirist to write. In the words of Feinberg:

> There is reason to suppose that he chooses the exposing of
> immorality and hypocrisy as his subject matter not because he is
> a reformer, nor because he is especially interested in improving
> things. He may, and usually does, have little thought of alterna-
> tives or substitutes. He is obeying an irresistible impulse to show
> absurdities which he sees very clearly. Usually, his immediate
> purpose is to satirize, not to improve; his object in showing the

ridiculous is to criticize, not to correct. . . . His primary purpose
is to satirize.

The satirist, then, functions as an artist, not as a moralist, using
for his material the moral values accepted by his society because
satire deals with deviations from a norm—an actual or pretended
norm (pp. 40–41).

That the satirist is motivated primarily by an aesthetic drive and only
secondarily by morality, revenge, frustrated idealism, or self-criticism
is quite possibly valid in the classical or even historical sense. But the
Soviet satirist's work within the tradition of Russian literature is a
different situation. Since the time of Gogol, through the catalysts of the
Radical Critics, the Natural School of nineteenth-century realism, and
the democratically minded Populists (excepting perhaps the Modernist
movement), Russian literature had established a tradition of social
consciousness and social involvement. Literature was used to combat
and polemicize against social, moral, and political ills. It is highly
probable that the Soviet satirist, especially the strongly proregime
satirist, was writing primarily to establish a certain political, social, or
moral norm and to defame its counterpart. Certainly Russian artists
who were primarily satirists throughout their careers, for example
Zoshchenko and Bulgakov, and who maintained high literary requirements for themselves were more likely to be motivated in the "higher,
classical" sense. But it should be pointed out that satire was written in
great abundance during the decade, much of it by writers who wrote
one or two satirical works specifically to show either the supremacy of
communism or the problems it brought and who then quickly turned to
other ventures. It would be folly to ask a satirist not to have a definite
point of view or even not to defend a particular system. But one has the
right to expect of the satirical artist a certain distance, detachment, or
objectivity. Again quoting Feinberg: "The satirist is likely to be skeptical about most social institutions. Even satirists who are staunch parti-
sans of specific political systems do not pretend that those systems are
perfect. . . the satirist is an attacker rather than a defender" (p. 253).

Perhaps the final major contribution of the period of War Communism to the development of satire in the twenties was the rebirth of
the literary language, which originated with Alexey Remizov, Andrey
Bely, Yevgeny Zamyatin, and the Futurist movement: "These attempts
[experiments in language and technique] followed two courses: linguistic play, which included all sorts of neologisms, twists of syntax, and
grammatical structure; and colloquial and vernacular speech. The

former exhausted itself and faded out by the 1930s; the second, however, showed more resistance. The first current gave rise to 'ornamental' prose, in which writers indulged in all kinds of verbal vignettes and embellishments, mainly borrowed from the modes of poetic language. This runs through most outstanding writers of the 1920s from Vsevolod Ivanov to Leonov, but thins out in the era of the five-year plans and loses its vigor—spontaneously or under blows from the outside. On the other hand, beginning with Mayakovsky's verse, written in the idiom of the streets and the mass meeting, Russian literature felt the tremendous impact of the vernacular."[10] These experiments made a rich addition to all literature during the decade. The most important effect on satire was the enrichment of the *skaz* technique. The major historical source of this technique was the nineteenth-century writer Nikolay Leskov, whose method has been defined by Hugh McLean as "stylistically individualized inner narrative placed in the mouth of a fictional character and designed to produce the illusion of oral speech."[11] The skaz provided an excellent method of characterizing the speaker, who was usually the traditional "little man." The speaker found many things beyond his understanding because of the complexities of the new Soviet life and because of his own naiveté. Such a character was ready-made for *ostranenie* (the device of estrangement used to alter perspective) and was usually someone who had not been changed or even affected by the Revolution. Thus, Fellow Traveler and emigré satirists were able to assert on the one hand that the Revolution had really changed nothing and on the other that it had succeeded only in confusing the common people. The outstanding practitioner of the device and of the many-faceted vernacular was Mikhail Zoshchenko.

The groundwork laid during War Communism came to fruition during NEP, and it was during these years of economic experimentation and chaos that satire truly flourished. Longer prose works dominated the literary output and took the place of the shorter publicistic works and feuilletons. However, with the development of what may be called the literary feuilleton it became rather difficult to distinguish this form from the short story, which flourished under the pens of major satirists such as Zoshchenko, Kataev, and Petrov and minor writers such as Vasily Lebedev-Kumach and Sven (pseudonym of Ilya Kremlev). The chronicle-povest continued to develop with a more involved plot and at least three excellent examples were produced: Konstantin Fedin's *Narovchatskaya khronika* (*Narovchatskaya Chronicle*); Leonid

Leonov's *Zapisi nekotorykh epizodov, sdelannye v gorode Gogulyove
Andreem Petrovichem Kovyakinym* (*Notes on Some Episodes Perpetrated in the City of Gogulyov by Andrey Petrovich Kovyakin*); and
Alexey Tolstoy's *Pokhozhdenia Nevzorova, ili Ibikus* (*The Adventures
of Nevzorov, or Ibikus*), in which the element of the picaresque hero
was added. The demand for more plot, such as *Ibikus* supplied to the
chronicle-povest, was a general trend during NEP. As a result, the
social utopian novel which Zamyatin had pioneered became infused
with more action and took its place alongside the adventure novel that
came into existence upon the request of the party. Valentin Kataev's
Ostrov Erendorf (*Erendorf Island*) was written in response to this
request. In an interview in 1962 with the author (used as a preface to a
new edition of the novel), Kataev explained the requisition: "The idea
for this novel arose as a result of an appeal in literature to create a
Soviet adventure novel. Marietta Shaginyan wrote at this time the
novel trilogy *Mess Mend, or the Yankees in Petrograd, Laurie Lane—
the Metal Worker*, and *The Road to Bagdad*. Valentin Kataev recalls:
'In the publishing department it was thought that newspapers were
poorly read in the provinces. It was decided to serialize high adventure
novels. They searched for writers. Sergey Ingulov tapped me and other
Southern Russian writers. I wrote *Erendorf Island* and they liked it.
The novel is satirical.' "[12]

Yury Olesha's *Tri tolstyaka* (*Three Fat Men*) is another example of
the trend toward plot in the novel. Zamyatin's "reactionary," satirical,
utopian novel *We* was followed by more "revolutionary" examples
during NEP, including Anatoly Shishko's *Appetit mikrobov* (*The Mi-
crobes' Appetite*), Yakov Okunev's *Katastrofa* (*The Catastrophe*), and
A. Lunacharskaya's *Gorod prosypaetsya* (*The City Awakes*). Agitprop
also continued to prosper and gained in intensity through Mayakovsky
and the Window of Satire of ROSTA.

Some new villains and satirical archetypes were added to the gallery
during NEP, the most important being the "Nepman," whose speculation, seeking for advantage, and pretentiousness were lampooned in-
cessantly. The Nepman, the survivors of the tsarist regime, and the
philistine proved to be the most popular and the safest targets. In
1923–24 another archetype came to the fore when embezzlement
became a problem of national consequence. In addition to the many
feuilletons addressing the problem, a number of longer prose works
appeared, among them Vladimir Lidin's *Rastrata Glotova* (*The Embezzlement of Glotov*), L. Grabar's *Lakhudrin pereulok* (*Lakhudrin Lane*),

Ilya Ehrenburg's *Rvach* (*The Racketeer*), and Valentin Kataev's *The Embezzlers*.

A factor in expanding the gallery of archetypes during NEP was the change in emphasis around 1924–25, when contemporary society became the chief concern of satirists who five years earlier had concentrated on the past, the Revolution, and the Civil War. The Revolution remained a vital theme throughout the decade, but after 1925 and into the initial stages of the first Five-Year Plan it played a decidedly secondary role to everyday life and living conditions. This change in emphasis indicates that many writers were coming to terms with the present and had abandoned their preoccupation with the past. The change was prompted not only by the time span between 1925 and the Revolution but, more important, by the sober reality of contemporary life, which had not yet attained the paradisiacal glory promised by October. The Fellow Travelers and emigrés indicted the system and blamed the Revolution for the poor quality of life; the proregime camp attempted to explain conditions by exposing remnants of the past and foreign capitalists and bourgeois who were working to sabotage those gains already made and to prevent new ones. Only toward the end of NEP was it admitted that the new system itself had produced some undesirable elements and that it was no longer justifiable to blame all of the problems on the past and on outsiders.

Essentially the same trends continued through the first two years of the first Five-Year Plan. The satirical novel and tale were the principal genres, although the short story and literary feuilleton continued to be important. In addition to the prime targets of NEP—remnants of the past, foreign imperialists and bourgeois, Nepmen, and the philistine—there was added another satirical archetype, the enemy of the Five-Year Plan, who could be anything from the foreign saboteur to the provincial kulak.

Throughout these three periods from the October Revolution through the first Five-Year Plan, there periodically surfaced a polemic over the fate of satire in a time of building a new way of life. Satire's right to exist was questioned, as were the terms of existence should the mode be permitted to continue. In 1923 a request that satire be used to combat social ills was met by a response that such themes as the bureaucrat were inappropriate to satire. The question quickly became one of what the satirist should be—the petty observer of social trivia or the giant of literary antiquity who combatted evil. Such arguments smoldered until 1927, when there was an official call for new Soviet

Gogols and Saltykovs. This resulted in a response from Gorky that the negative in society should be beaten down with laughter rather than simple exposé with an appended moral.[13] Discussions of the problem followed in *Literaturnaya gazeta (Literary Gazette)* in 1929 and 1930. A critical issue was raised in January 1930 by the critic V. Blyum, who insisted that since satire must have antagonists and since Soviet society had no class antagonism, then the idea of Soviet satire was as outdated as that of a Soviet banker. There could be no heritage from Gogol or Saltykov in Soviet times. Newspapers responded with the strong view that satire was indeed a proper activity for the masses in correcting social ills. It is ironic that this very justification for satire led to its demise, as satirists marshaled themselves during the first Five-Year Plan to serve the state by exposing and correcting ills.

Choosing to end the discussion at or near the close of the decade is somewhat arbitrary, but by 1930 the country was well into the first Five-Year Plan and the government was beginning to assert itself more strongly in the control of literature. The dominance of the Russian Association of Proletarian Writers (RAPP), before it was purged by the party, brought tremendous pressure to bear on the Fellow Travelers, the group of writers that produced most of the lasting contributions to Russian and Soviet literature. Many of these writers were eventually silenced or forced to direct their talents into ventures less objectionable to the government: Zamyatin emigrated; Bulgakov asked to work in the theater and kept his most devastating indictment of the system, *Master i Margarita (The Master and Margarita)*, in manuscript form; Olesha left the field of literature after attempting to write ideologically acceptable material; Zoshchenko came under periodic criticism. The death of Mayakovsky and the party's demand for relevance in literature to meet the needs of socialization and collectivization also contributed to stunting the growth of satire.

The creation of the monolithic Union of Soviet Writers in 1932 and the purges of the middle and late thirties sounded the death knell for satire and showed that censorship and restrictions can indeed blunt the satirical pen. The thirties were bleak: "Toward the end of the 1930s satirical books were at any rate published. But what kind? The satires of Juvenal were issued in a new translation ('Academia,' 1937); the *Selected Epigrams* of Martialis (Goslitizdat, 1937); and finally there appeared Ilf and Petrov's book of satirical-humoristic sketches about America. Not a single satirical novel or story dealing directly with contemporary material was written with the exception of L. Lagin's humorous adventure tale for children *Old Man Khottabych* (1938)."[14] The theme of contemporary life remained, but it was defined in a utilitarian manner in the thirties. Government projects became more important than living conditions and the inequities and paradoxes of Soviet life.

Satire revived during the war years but was largely confined to political journalism in the hands of Alexey Tolstoy, Leonid Leonov, Mikhail Sholokhov, Demyan Bedny, Samuil Marshak, Ilya Ehrenburg, and Sergey Mikhalkov. The subsequent Zhdanov years again produced demands from the party and the Writers' Union for new Gogols and Saltykovs, but none was readily forthcoming. Despite periodic thaws in the literary atmosphere since 1953, satire has yet to return to its flourishing condition of the twenties. The principal reason for this has been the party's attempt to apply the abstract and nebulous strictures of Socialist Realism to satire: "our satire, as differentiated from classical satire, must not be accusatory or castigating, but rather 'lyrically pathetic and positive.' "[15] The results have been damaging: "The most poignant social and moral problems have sunk to the level of the trivia of day-to-day life and disagreements in the spheres of trade and transport. The tendencies of prettifying life and minimizing contrasts and the attempt to brush aside the contradictions of reality have undermined the bases of satire."[16] The party's attempt to remove the unmasking aspect of satire eliminated not only one of the classical criteria for satire but also the flowering of its own satire.

2. The Revolution and the Civil War: Event and Effect

THE REVOLUTION and its effect on the people were treated satirically only by the Fellow Travelers and emigrés. Much of the exposé was bitter. These writers were as one-sided in their satirical portrayal of the vast upheaval as an evil and inept force as were the proregime writers in defending it as the dreaded reaper sweeping away the inequities of society and the enemies of the people. The satirical indictments of the Revolution were usually artistically more successful than the bandwagon eulogies written by its supporters, since the more capable writers were the Fellow Travelers. Many of the Fellow Travelers and emigrés initially accepted the February Revolution, for they did feel the need for reform. But when the Bolsheviks seized power and sanctified October, these writers quickly became disenchanted and did not hesitate to express their deep disappointment and bitterness.

One of the staunchest foes of the sanctification of October was Yevgeny Zamyatin, who applied his theory of revolution and entropy to all aspects of life. His work provided the initial satirical caricature of October. To Zamyatin, revolution in the sense of constant constructive change was an eternal principle and was the archenemy of entropy, which he defined as inertia and stagnation resulting from dogmatism. He satirized the official Soviet myths and the demand for conformity as producers of entropy. Zamyatin began his attack on entropy with *Ostrovityane (The Islanders)*, written in 1917 to satirize life as he had observed it in England. The mouthpiece for entropy in the work is Vicar Dooley, a clergyman who has worked out a system for compulsatory salvation:

> Vicar Dooley was of course that same Dooley who was the
> pride of Jesmond and the author of the book *The Testament of
> Compulsatory Salvation*. The schedules which had been drawn
> up consistent with the *Testament* were hung on the walls of Mr.
> Dooley's library. A schedule for eating; a schedule for repentance

18

(twice a week); a schedule for exercise and fresh air; a schedule for doing good works; and finally, amidst the others, one schedule, which out of modesty was untitled and which had special application to Mrs. Dooley, on which was noted every third Saturday.[1]

Dooley's strict outlay of his time and rigid conformity to his schedule ("life must become a well-oiled machine which leads us with mechanical inevitability to the desired goal")[2] serve as an introduction to *We* with its Table of Hours and absolute submission to the will of the state. *The Islanders* was prompted by Zamyatin's philosophical concern with entropy. His subsequent work during War Communism assumed a political bias and linked the Revolution and its resultant system with stagnation.

It is evident from *The Islanders* that Zamyatin viewed the established church as one of the forces of entropy, and he enlarged upon this attitude three years later with the publication of the historical drama "Ogni sv. Dominika" ("The Fires of St. Dominic") in 1920. The play is set in Seville during the Inquisition of the second half of the sixteenth century; it portrays the folly of an overly dogmatic approach to institutions, authority, and doctrine. The analogy between the Inquisition's eradication of enemies of the church and the Cheka's providing the same service for the new Soviet government is quite obvious. The play was immediately perceived as an allegory by Soviet critics and denounced as an attack upon the system. Several characters are satirized through their fanatical devotion to the church (and by analogy to the Soviet government or any other monolithic dogma). Don Baltasar surrenders his brother Don Ruy to the Inquisitor with this comment:

> But he [Ruy] must understand that the work of the Inquisition is the work of the church, and because of this it is an honor for each of us! (Banging his fist on the table.) Isn't it obvious that murder, lying, anything you like for the sake of the church is more noble than the most noble exploit for Satan and his servants the heretics?[3]

And Brother Pedro, one of the priests working in the Inquisition, expresses pity for the independent mind of Don Ruy:

> Such an unhappy one! If the church told me that I had only one eye, I would agree even with that; I would come to believe even in that. Because even though I know very well that I have two eyes, I know even more assuredly that the church cannot be mistaken.[4]

Zamyatin demonstrates in "The Fires of St. Dominic" that the results of such comic and blind devotion are tragic. People become subhuman caricatures: Baltasar willingly sacrifices his brother; Dominican monks hunt heretics as if they were animals; observers scream for blood when the heretics are marched into the square to be burned and then revel in their death. The principles of Christianity become distorted, as is evident in a conversation between two soldiers:

> And then, señor, His Majesty the king answered this way: "If my own son turned out to be a heretic, I would be the first to set fire to his bonfire." Aren't those words worthy of a true Christian?[5]

Absolute devotion and sanctification produce perversion of the original principles, and institutions and ideas are substituted for people and human values. Zamyatin's initial conclusion concerning the entropy of October was quickly amplified by many Fellow Travelers and emigrés. Of all Zamyatin's work, *We* displays most poignantly the consequences of entropy. Vicar Dooley's desire to function like a machine in mechanized surroundings is developed into the creation of dehumanized automatons appropriately called Numbers in *We*, the first example in Soviet satire of the technique of mass reduction. The links with the Revolution are many and unflattering. The United State is the analogue of Soviet Russia, and the intentions of the Revolution in both are expressed in the commission given to D–503:

> You have an even more glorious feat to perform: to integrate the eternal equation of the universe with the glassy, electrical fire-breathing INTEGRAL. You must subordinate to the beneficent yoke of reason the unknown beings living on other planets, who are perhaps still in the primitive state of freedom. If they fail to understand that we are bringing them mathematically infallible happiness, our goal is to force them to be happy. But we will use words before we use weapons.[6]

For Zamyatin, the Revolution is the harbinger of the future paradise but only on its own terms, for it determines both the method of establishment and the kind of paradise to be instituted. The method of establishment is a sequence of Revolution, sanctification, and forcible imposition, a process ridiculed by Zamyatin through one of the naive statements of D–503: "Well then, if we focus in on the idea of 'right,' even with ancient peoples the more mature knew that the source of right is might. Right is a function of might."[7] D–503 is thus a derivative of Vicar Dooley, who regarded force as an integral ingredient of his plan:

> If the government stagnates in its resolve and neglects its obligations, then we, all of us, must force our neighbors along the path of salvation, drive them with scorpions, drive them like slaves. It will be better for them to be slaves of God than free sons of Satan. . . .[8]

Zamyatin portrays the enforced paradise in absurdly comical terms, and *We* marks one of the rare instances during the decade of the extensive use of the ludicrous. Humor was particularly lacking in the treatment of the Revolution, which was for the most part regarded vindictively and soberly by the Fellow Travelers and emigrés. The ludicrous elements in D–503's paradise include the naive statements about saving men from the shackles of freedom; the Bureau of Guardians (the analogue of the Cheka) and the guardians themselves, who remind D–503 of guardian angels; the multiplication tables used to determine birth; the worship of the *Blagodetel* (the Benefactor) as a combined god and political virtuoso (a comment upon the organizers of the Revolution); the depersonalization of each resident by a number; the surgical procedure to remove fantasy; the state requirement of fifty chews per bite of food, done to the beat of soothing yet mechanical music; and the Table of Hours, which partially achieves Vicar Dooley's ideal of mechanized life but which is as yet imperfect because of the personal hours. Again Zamyatin uses the comic naiveté of his narrator to satirize the Revolution and its goals, this time referring to the personal hours:

> But I firmly believe—let them call me an idealist and a fantasizer—I believe that sooner or later, but eventually, we will find a place in the general formula even for these hours. Eventually all 86,400 seconds will fit into the Table of Hours.[9]

Zamyatin's use of D–503 as his narrator is attributable to both the skaz technique and the novel-diary. D–503's journal brings the narrative to a first-person plane and accomplishes the in-depth characterization of the narrator, which is the principal purpose of the novel-diary. Historically the novel-diary was frequently the vehicle of either sentimental love stories or psychological investigations. Skaz usually reflected a naive, provincial narrator and the approximation of oral, often quite colloquial, speech. Thus, skaz was a linguistic device using colorful dialectal, ungrammatical speech to parallel the equally colorful actions of the narrator, who often casts fresh light on institutions, customs, and people unfamiliar to him. D–503 is an educated man whose journal is quite removed from oral speech, which thus has no linguistic effect. Nevertheless, D–503 is a descendant of the uninitiated provincial whose naive and comical statements characterize himself and expose the frightening absurdity of the monolithic state and its devotees.

Zamyatin's development from *The Islanders* through "The Fires of St. Dominic" to *We*, evident in the application of his theory of entropy and revolution to contemporary politics, indicates the direction satire followed after October. Satirists of all political persuasions related themselves to, wrote about, and equated all aspects of contemporary life to politics. Zamyatin was one of the first to do so; he was instrumental in the initiation and development of the satire of the Fellow Travelers but differed from them in one major way: he was a philosopher of sorts in addition to being an artist, and in his works he waged ideological warfare with the new system from a well-defined point of view. Fellow Traveler satirists opposed the Soviet regime ideologically, but their point of departure was not a philosophical system. Zamyatin's philosophical base was the primary source of his opposition to the Soviet government, and in this sense he was the only satirist who attempted to combat Marxism in the arena of philosophy.

The prompt and vigorous critical response to "The Fires of St. Dominic" and *We* and Zamyatin's ultimate fate were prophetic. Already by 1920 criticism and censorship were easily provoked, and Zamyatin was the first satirist singled out for criticism because of his treatment of the Revolution. His use of allegory failed to prevent denunciation even in the years of comparative freedom. The example of Zamyatin indicated to the Fellow Travelers the perils of their ideological position. Nevertheless, they, like the emigrés, remained largely on the level of the obvious in their treatment of October during the period of War Communism, and it was only later in the decade that allegory was again employed.

Zamyatin's influence on satire in the twenties was by no means confined to his treatment of the Revolution. His role in the development of the utopian genre has already been mentioned, but he exercised a more personal literary influence as an informal mentor of the Serapion Brothers, whose membership numbered Mikhail Zoshchenko, among others. His experiments with the skaz influenced the development of Zoshchenko; his development of so-called microscopic realism was a critical factor in the career of Yury Olesha; his experimentation with various verbal and compositional modernistic prose techniques affected Boris Pilnyak and the young Leonid Leonov. Indeed, together with Alexey Remizov and Andrey Bely, Zamyatin was one of the decisive stylistic influences on all prose of the twenties, and many used his methods and devices.

Mikhail Bulgakov, like Zamyatin a Fellow Traveler, and possibly the outstanding satirist of the decade, also exposed the Revolution but was not dominated by an overriding *Weltanschauung* as was Zamyatin. He treats October in *Heart of a Dog*, wherein the operation performed on the stray dog Sharik is an allegory of the Revolution. Professor Preobrazhensky transplants the testes and pituitary gland of a drunken, balalaika-playing thief into the dog. The professor, portrayed as if he were a priest performing some mysterious rite, represents a Lenin-Trotsky figure who engineers the Revolution. (It will be remembered that Zamyatin's Benefactor in *We* is also treated as a religious figure.) The patient quickly develops into Poligraf Poligrafovich Sharikov, the new Soviet man, who at best is portrayed as a reprehensible mutt. It is significant that before the operation Sharik could be termed a "good dog," but his combination with a criminal element produces a disaster. Preobrazhensky himself becomes so disenchanted with his creation that he performs the operation in reverse, and Sharikov quickly reverts back to Sharik. For Bulgakov the Revolution is an experiment disrupting the natural evolution of people, institutions, and events. It is a singular failure, but it is a mistake that can be corrected. The mistake results from the whim of a "mad scientist," whose perception of reality is not clouded by devotion to his own theories and experiments. Hence October is not an absolute, and is unable to demand fanatical devotion. In fact, according to Bulgakov, October has little influence upon those who do not care to be influenced or who see to the core of its reality. Bulgakov's portrayal of the Revolution is much more typical of Fellow Traveler satirists than is Zamyatin's, although Zamyatin's technical influence was greater. Fellow Travelers on the whole tended to mock the Revolution using Bulgakov's criteria.

The satirical depiction of the Revolution was naturally common among the emigrés, where a dominant note of bitterness relegated humor to a secondary role. For example, Alexey Remizov in *Vzvi-khryonnaya Rus (Turbulent Russia)* describes October as "The very thing, which without 'tactical considerations,' without 'after all, it's war time,' without 'the point of view of the masses,' is simply called murder, treachery, baseness"; in *V rozovom bleske (On a Field Azure)*, he comments, "and thus [the Revolution] began its metallic work, breaking and crushing vital human life without a single thought for man."[10] Remizov lamented the passing of ancient Russia and indicted the Revolution for the hurt and suffering rampant among the people who had been forcibly torn from religion, tradition, and native soil. Remizov's portrayal of the forcible imposition of the new order is reminiscent of Zamyatin's interpretation of October as a movement valuing theories and change above human life.

A similar stance was assumed by Ivan Shmelyov, who castigated the Revolution in a number of short stories written in the first few years of the decade. *Dva Ivana: Istoria (Two Ivans: A History)* depicts the different ideological and philosophical approaches of two men, one who supports the Revolution enthusiastically and the other who becomes a successful speculator. Each accuses the other and his point of view of being responsible for Russia's troubles, but ironically both suffer and ultimately perish because of October. Thus the Revolution is a deceiving force, destroying even its adherents. This same concept is expressed in the story *Oryol (The Eagle)*. The narrator, Ivan Bebeshin, a sailor who had served on the "Aurora" at the outset of the Revolution, states:

> Something is all out of kilter. They announced that now Russia had become a peasant and worker and Soviet place, but you can't see the Russian government anywhere, and there is no equality, and they're against God. And it isn't even Russia, it's some kind of "Russian Soviet Federative Socialist Republic." The sons of bitches, they deceived us. And this really burns me up![11]

The emigré writer who made the most extensive and militant use of the satirical mode against October was Arkady Averchenko. Primarily a humorist while still in Russia, Averchenko in emigration often indulged himself in a kind of agitprop campaign against the Revolution and against the well-known individuals responsible for it. The primary vehicle of his satire was a combination of the literary feuilleton, the short story, and the sketch, all cast in a low humor. The best examples of this vehicle are in a collection called *Dyuzhina nozhey v spinu revolyutsii* (*A Dozen Knives in the Revolution's Back*). In his preface to the collection Averchenko expresses feelings quite typical for many who emigrated. While recognizing the necessity for reform and the positive first steps of the February Revolution, he vociferously denounces the events during and following October as having nothing in common with a true revolution:

> Surely you don't think that the rot, stupidity, rubbish, soot, and gloom that is going on now is really a revolution?
>
> A revolution is a beautiful flash of sparkling lightning; a revolution is the beatifically beautiful face of wrathful Fate; a revolution is a blindingly bright rocket arcing like a rainbow through the dank gloom! . . .
>
> Do current events recall these glittering images?. . .
>
> [comparing the Revolution to the birth and development of a child] . . . when at four years of age the child utters such inarticulate, senseless words like "*sovnarkhoz, uezemelkom, sovbur*, and *revvoenkom*," then this is not the touching, caressing eye of a child, but, forgive me, a rather decent lad who has fallen into a reserved idiocy.
>
> Quite often, however, this reserved idiocy turns into the violent kind and then the child is totally unmanageable![12]

Averchenko devoted himself to the depiction of the violent idiocy and was the source for much of the bitter and accusatory tone characterizing emigré satire on the Revolution.

October ultimately became a composite of images and attitudes found in the work of Zamyatin, Bulgakov, Shmelyov, and Averchenko. Zamyatin contributed the image of the monolith that abused personal freedom yet received an intense devotion. The Revolution produced a negative utopia that threatened to engulf and destroy all in its path. Bulgakov mocked the Revolution as a mistake and did not endow it with an aura of irreversible horror and invincibility. He added the figure of the new Soviet man who was little more than a criminal grafted artificially onto society and who successfully complemented Zamyatin's dehumanized automaton. Shmelyov accused the makers of the Revolution of deception and failure to keep campaign promises. He resented the disavowal of traditional values and indicted October for destroying but not creating. Averchenko used the romance and accomplishments of real revolutions to expose the excesses of October. The composite of these images and ideas did not survive the decade because of political pressure, and even within the decade it assumed a role secondary in importance to the satirical portrayal of the effect of the Revolution on society and on the common man.

The satirical portrayal of the Revolution's effect on society encompassed three principal points: deprivation and poor living conditions, particularly during War Communism; the common man's lack of understanding and superficial acceptance of the new order; and the absence of substantive change in people or institutions.

Shmelyov and Averchenko made the most significant quantitative contribution to the satirical description of the living conditions resulting from the Revolution. Shmelyov's most bitter indictment of the Revolution is found in *Solntse myortvykh* (*The Sun of the Dead*), a record of his own stay in the Crimea during the worst of War Communism, from 1918 until he emigrated in 1922.[13] Communism and the event of the Revolution itself are noticeably absent from the work; instead, the novelist examines the Revolution's consequences. He shows that those living in the Crimea sank to the level of cavemen and animals, making clear that the Revolution had a regressive rather than a constructive effect, destroying people rather than producing a paradise. Reminiscent of Zamyatin, Shmelyov describes those who formulated the socialist gospel as indifferent to humanity and irresponsible. They place their great Experiment above everything and allow the masses to starve while announcing to the world that all is well. The proclaimed paradise is therefore meant only for the direct participants in the Revolution, while the majority of the people are either excluded or ignore the changes and are exploited:

> And on the tables lay packets of papers which toward evening were marked with a red letter . . . one fateful letter. Two precious words begin with this letter: *Rodina* [Fatherland] and *Russia. Raskhod* [expenditure] and *rasstrel* [execution] also begin with this letter. Those who go out to kill are not aware of either the Fatherland or Russia. This is now obvious.[14]

A note of sentimentality verging on melodrama was added to the prevailing bitterness and derision. Shmelyov's melodrama results from his deep personal hurt at the loss of his son and from humanitarian indignation, while Averchenko, a more superficial writer, employed melodrama as a castigating device. For effect, he frequently used the image of starving people and suffering children, and he considered irreparable the damage wrought by October. For Averchenko and other emigrés the Revolution was simply an excuse for many to plunder and use violence, and as long as the principles of the Revolution were in force the circumstances of life would not improve appreciably.

N. A. Teffi produced one of the most successful emigré satires on the results of the Revolution in the story *Tonkie pisma* (*Subtle Letters*), in which her usual light humor assumes a more raucous note. In the tale an emigré living in Paris receives a strange letter from his brother in Russia, who expresses great delight that he and his acquaintances are all dying of hunger or have been killed. The emigré composes a reply expressing horror that affairs are in such a state, but a friend advises him that such a letter cannot be sent:

> First of all you must write as if you were a woman, otherwise they will shoot your brother as the brother of one who fled from the draft. In the second place you should not mention that you received his letter, because correspondence is forbidden. And then you must not show that you know how miserable they live.

Armed with this information the emigrant pens a new letter:

> Dear Volodya!
>
> I didn't get your letter. It's great that all is going so well with you. Is it really true that people have stopped eating human flesh! That's charming! Be careful! They say that you have a terrible birth rate. All of this dreadfully comforts us. I am doing poorly. If you were only here, it would really be miserable. I married a Frenchman and it's awful.
>
> Your sister,
Ivan
>
> P.S. All of you go to the devil! Teffi.[15]

It is evident that the image of the Revolution from the pens of non-Communist writers was almost always negative, or at least skeptical, and that when the satirical mode was employed a bitter and accusatory note dominated. Bitterness led the emigrés to a one-sided portrayal of the aftermath of the Revolution. They attributed the trying conditions of War Communism to the Revolution and depicted a great disparity between the lives of the average citizen and the revolutionary. Implicit in this disparity is that the Revolution with its new leaders and ideology ignored the welfare of the people, imposed abusive regulations, and established a paradise for only the few.

Proregime satirists made light of the old malcontents who adopted this ridiculing stance and who blamed every social ill on the Revolution. A stereotyped character who harbored these attitudes quickly emerged: these self-appointed social critics and philosophers are all remnants of tsardom, usually old men who have a very unattractive physical appearance and who try to disrupt the functioning of the new order. A typical example is Valentin Kataev's *Starik Sabakin* (*Old Man Sabakin*), an emigré in spirit, who comments, "The sons of bitches! The people have become lax! Cads! They have no moral principles! Hooliganism everywhere you look. The Soviet government, that's what it is. Yes sir!" and who is described quite appropriately as having a "short, gray crew cut, a fat nose, violet ears, drawn cheeks, and small malicious eyes deeply and solidly lodged under a narrow, wrinkled forehead."[16] It is noteworthy that both Bulgakov and Kataev used the image of the dog to help portray the satirized character in a subhuman light.

The satirical portrayal of the day-to-day effects of the Revolution upon the people, apart from the largely economic considerations of War Communism, was the exclusive province of the Fellow Travelers and emigrés. Proregime writers did approach the subject in an indirect way by exposing remnants of the past and figures flourishing during NEP as those who refused, for either selfish or devious purposes, to submit themselves to the will of the people. The writers' view was that a small number of people, the negative force, had not accepted October, the positive force. In the works of Fellow Traveler and emigré satirists, however, the Revolution was accused of the most serious of failings: the people themselves did not understand it and there had been no real change produced by it. Proregime writers faulted individuals for the failure of the Revolution to take hold in certain areas, while Fellow Travelers saw the failings inherent in the ideology and practice of the Revolution itself.

Zamyatin's *Slovo prinadlezhit tovarishchu Churyginu* (*Comrade Churygin Has the Floor*) demonstrates the peasants' total lack of understanding of the Revolution. In the story some peasants march to the estate of a rich landowner to demand to know what is happening following the death of their champion, Rasputin. While they are questioning the landowner, another peasant arrives with news of the Revolution:

> The tsar in the person of Nikolay has been replaced, and all kinds of nasty palaces have to be wiped off the face of the earth so there won't be any more rich people, and we'll all live like poor proletarians just like in the Bible, only now it's because of the science of our beloved Marx.[17]

All the peasants rejoice at the news, ironically in the name of Orthodoxy, and they are bewildered that according to Marx religion is
considered superstition. In keeping with the Revolution they decide to
destroy the estate and begin with a Roman statue, but the landowner
objects, asserting that the statue is a very costly replica of Mars.
Confusing it with Marx, the peasants remove their caps and pay it
homage. These events are related through the skaz technique in the
guise of a speech given by Churygin at a party meeting. Churygin
blames the mistakes of Rasputin and Mars on the peasants' ignorance,
but he remains baffled by the new ideology and way of life. Zamyatin
mocks the fact that even though October was perpetrated in the name
of peasants and workers, the peasants know little about it and understand still less.

Comrade Churygin Has the Floor and later *Ix (Ex)* differ markedly from Zamyatin's earlier work. By the middle twenties he had
departed from the concept of the horrible, all-powerful state
which forcibly imposed its will, turning men into machines. The
negative utopia of "The Fires of St. Dominic" and *We* gave way
to the practical influence and implementation of October in a contemporary setting. October, once almost omnipotent in Zamyatin's
works, is now shrouded in superficiality and ineptitude and bears
little resemblance to the United State. The Soviet system and the
event of October itself exhibit lethargic entropy, the result of
stagnant revolution. It is significant that the ideology and setting
of such stories are consistent with the bulk of Fellow Traveler satire in mid-decade.

The second contention used to belittle the influence of the Revolution was the superficial conviction and lack of understanding the common people had in the principles of the new order. Frequently this
conviction went little deeper than slogans, and specific issues were
regarded lackadaisically. The stories of Zoshchenko feature many
examples of the superficial acceptance of the new order. The average
man's enthusiasm and ideological steadfastness become a function of
his physical well-being in the years of deprivation. In the story
Tochnaya ideologia (An Exact Ideology) some workers are accused of
not having a precise ideology, and Seryozha Blokhin, a minor office
worker, stands to refute the statement. He stammers, however, and is
unable to say anything, thereby verifying the accusation. On the way
home he rehearses what he should have said and then repeats it to his
wife, assuring her that it was part of a dynamic speech he made in

defense of the workers. Blokhin utters such ideologically pregnant statements as "We can, I say, sacrifice our lives on the altar of the Fatherland should the government need it," and "Life, I say, is fine, but truth, I say, is more important."[18] This elevated social consciousness endures only until Blokhin is informed that his rent has been raised. He explodes and goes to the house manager, whom he loudly berates until the rate is lowered. To paraphrase his remarks, ideological relevance is fine but one's own well-being is more important. Zoshchenko was the most prominent of the Fellow Travelers in portraying the domestic sphere. His assertion that the average man's devotion to communism was based only on clichés and a deceptive external allegiance and that the citizens' basic concerns and motivations had in no way been affected was made a maxim by Fellow Traveler satirists.

The third part of the indictment of October was that there was no real change. This was possibly the most serious, inasmuch as simple people could conceivably be educated in the new ideology and deprivation could be remedied (even though Fellow Traveler and emigré satirists disputed both possibilities), but the cataclysmic force of the Revolution should produce immediate changes in people, institutions, and the very structure of society. In *Turbulent Russia*, Remizov reacted to the lack of change and typified the tone for Fellow Traveler and emigré approaches to the issue:

> It's good when a storm comes, but I don't think that man will change: he'll be the same in his grave as he was at birth. I know that the most turbulent storm of all, the revolution, screaming and shaking, will not change a thing, but I also know that without a storm all is lost.
> People haven't changed at all. All over the earth it is threatening, threatening them! But just like before they babble all kinds of nonsense and have absolutely no notion that there is something approaching. And it is uncertain how all of this will end.[19]

People tend not to change, and the Revolution has no power to compel them. This portrayal counters Zamyatin's initial view of the future, in which men are forcibly transformed into mechanized servants of the state. When dealing with the Revolution's ultimate effect, Fellow Traveler and emigré satirists preferred to present October more in the guise of a harmless devil than of a fearsome creation.

The lack of change was best evidenced by the retention of pre-

October habits, attitudes, and ideals, particularly those traits and institutions which bore the brunt of concerted propaganda efforts. One of the most onerous for the proregime satirist was the retention of religious mannerisms, habits, and customs. Satirical characters frequently cross themselves, make oaths in the name of Deity, and use religious terminology, particularly during comic moments of crisis when they are most likely to return to those habits most deeply ingrained. The celebration of religious holidays was also continued. This practice was the subject of Valentin Kataev's *Pervomayskaya Paskha (A May Day Easter)*. Kukuev, the president of the local labor council, invites several guests for the Easter celebration, which happens to coincide with the May Day commemoration. *Khristos voskrese* ("Christ is risen!") is cordially exchanged among the guests according to long-standing tradition. But a party official arrives unexpectedly to help Kukuev celebrate May Day and comments "What in the world is going on here, brother? Isn't this an Easter table? Religious superstitions? Petty bourgeois guests? Ay-yay-yay! I didn't expect this from you even though you aren't a Party member!"[20] Kukuev hurriedly asserts that the party is really a meeting called to discuss production. The letters *Kh. V. (Khristos voskrese)* are explained as *Khozyaystvennoe Vozrozhdenie* (economic regeneration) and the various food items are referred to as production samples. After further explanation, the sampling of food energetically begins.

Kataev's treatment of the lack of change was typical of one approach taken by the proregime camp. The indicator of this lack of change is a non-Communist type who is exposed comically and who is juxtaposed with a Communist. The party and those satirists who supported it were willing to admit that the Revolution had not yet reached everyone, but they indicated that those who remained untouched did so because of traits that the Revolution had for the most part eradicated and not because of inadequacies inherent in October. Proregime satirists showed that only in the case of isolated individuals was the Revolution not efficacious. The Fellow Travelers and emigrés, in contrast, attempted to universalize October's inability to reach the masses, and they emphasized the retention of a pre-October life style.

Possibly the outstanding exposé of the superficial change in society is Bulgakov's *Pokhozhdenia Chichikova (The Adventures of Chichikov)*. As cited by Gleb Struve, the work successfully illustrates the ironic formula of Vasily Shulgin, an emigré journalist: "Everything the same, but slightly worse."[21] The illustration of the formula is accomplished principally through the echo of Gogol's *Myortvye dushi* (*Dead Souls*). Soviet writers and critics for the most part interpreted Gogol as a social critic and viewed *Dead Souls* as an indictment of tsardom, serfdom, and the civil service. Consequently, Bulgakov's application of the novel to Soviet life was immediately recognized for what it was—a satirical depiction of the superficial changes produced by October and a mockery of the system that professed to have changed the very core of life. As Chichikov returns to twentieth-century Russia, even the overt changes are negligible. His entrance into the same hotel in which he stayed almost one hundred years before illustrates the lack of change:

> Everything in the hotel was exactly the same as it was before: cockroaches were peeping out of the crevices, and it even seemed that there were more of them. But there were some changes too. For example, instead of the sign "Hotel" there hung a poster with the inscription "Hostel No. Such and Such," and, needless to say, there was such dirt and filth that even Gogol couldn't have imagined.[22]

Chichikov is able to succeed in Soviet society through his personal charm and manners as he had done before, and he finds that he is still able to use his cunning to get ahead. The irony evident in the remarkable success and notoriety enjoyed by an avowed capitalist in the Soviet state is indicative of the superficiality of applied socialism. Not only is Chichikov welcomed enthusiastically, but everywhere he goes he sees refugees from *Dead Souls*: a Sobakevich eats like a pig and maneuvers to secure goods for nothing; a Nozdryov leads a profligate life and lies uncontrollably; and a Korobochka is duped into buying part of Moscow. The Soviet citizenry are no different than the personified vices of Gogol's novel, and Soviet life provides a fertile playground for their antics. Once again Chichikov is exposed by a drunken Nozdryov, but the officials are unable to locate him, and Bobchinsky, a comic bumbler in Gogol's play "Revizor" ("The Inspector General"), is sent to look for him. Bobchinsky, the embodiment of the Soviet police, conducts a search and unearths still more Gogolian characters. At last Bulgakov himself volunteers to find Chichikov and solve the mystery but has to work through a Lyapkin-Tyapkin (the judge in "The Inspector General") to do it. The fact that the author makes such pointed use of Gogol recalls for the reader many assumptions about the nature of man and society and contributes much toward the satirical impact of the work.

Bulgakov's assertions that no substantial change for the better had occurred and that in fact the quality of life had regressed are consistent with his initial satirical interpretation of the event of October. The Revolution was a whim, a reversible experiment that did not command the total allegiance even of its instigators (compare Professor Preobrazhensky in *Heart of a Dog*). Its application to contemporary Russian life, therefore, was slipshod and was carried out with only half-serious devotion. Bulgakov emphasizes the external change, such as the dubbing of a hotel as hostel, and demonstrates the lack of substantive internal change. In this respect he reiterates Zoshchenko's generalizations about the allegedly new breed of Soviet citizen.

A further indication that nothing had really changed was the fact that certain individuals continued to live well while others remained in poverty, even after the trials of War Communism. Those who lived well were either those who had done so before the Revolution and who found that October brought little to interfere with their lives or else those members of the new Communist aristocracy who were as predatory and exploitative as those class enemies they had denounced and supposedly eradicated. While *The Adventures of Chichikov* garners much of its success and effect from literary allusions and humor, those works satirizing the continued inequality of living conditions were more chastising and less humorous. Many satirists felt that the only change the Revolution had wrought was that a new Communist aristocracy had taken the place of part of the old. The rationale for exposing these continuing inequities was different for each literary group and proceeded along the same lines as most politico-literary decisions. Proregime writers exposed the condition in order to attack aristocratic remnants of the past and bad examples of communism, while the Fellow Travelers and emigrés wanted to show the ultimate futility of the Revolution, thereby illustrating Shulgin's formula. The chronicle-povest was particularly effective in demonstrating the lack of real change because of its ability to show several years in perspective. A good example is Leonov's *Notes on a Few Episodes Perpetrated in the City of Gogulyov by Andrey Petrovich Kovyakin*, in which humor dominates until events and conditions turn sour after 1917. For Kovyakin and all others in the work, life is much worse after the Revolution than before. The chronicle ends on a note of definite melancholy, and there are no implications suggesting the possibility of any improvement.

The Revolution professed to be the political triumph of the proletariat and the harbinger of a workers' paradise. Averchenko's *Cherty iz zhizni rabochego Panteleya Grymzina* (*Characteristics of the Life of the Worker Panteley Grymzin*) shows that the Revolution produced no change even within the class it ostensibly represented. Panteley is just as destitute after the Revolution as he was under tsardom despite the realization of his desire that the workers rule. Conditions remain the same, and the Revolution is not only ineffectual but also deceptive because of its empty promises to the worker.

The Civil War

The satirical depiction of the Civil War is a direct outgrowth of the treatment of the Revolution, since the period of War Communism was viewed simply as the Revolution's attempt to establish itself. The Civil War provided targets for writers of all persuasions. The Fellow Travelers and emigrés concentrated on the figure of the Communist soldier and on life under the Bolsheviks during the Civil War. Proregime writers exposed the White movement, Western political leaders, and the politics of Allied intervention. In addition, both camps attacked the person and influence of Alexander Kerensky.

According to the Fellow Travelers and especially the emigrés, life under War Communism was characterized by deprivation of life's essentials, Bolshevik brutality, and the constant struggle for survival, all of which were the fault of the Communists. This picture of life appears in Zamyatin's *Mamay, Drakon* (*The Dragon*) and *Peshchera* (*The Cave*), Remizov's *Turbulent Russia*, and Boris Pilnyak's *Goly god* (*The Naked Year*), but the representation of the conditions and the intent of the works were not necessarily satirical. Writers from all ideological groups portrayed the deprivation during the Civil War, but most of them employed it as a background to convey an aura of romantic adventure or naturalism, and little genuine satire was written on the subject. Much irony but very little humor was visible under these conditions, and most writers chose to portray what could be called antilife.

The proregime satirists were not nearly so reticent and found much to ridicule. They mocked the White, both humorously and vindictively, and a stereotyped White quickly evolved. The White and the Communist are practically identical and could rather easily be interchanged. Both are characterized by brutality, ineptitude, and lack of feeling, and both emerge as nonhuman. The slavish devotion to the sanctity of October and the mechanized life of the Communist were exchanged for the aristocratic pretentiousness and selfishness of the Whites. The stereotype became so established, indeed required, that Bulgakov's *Belaya gvardia* (*The White Guard*) and "Dni Turbinykh" ("The Days of the Turbins"), which attempted to present the Whites as complex people rather than as stereotyped caricatures, were met with strong criticism and accusations of sympathy with the White cause.

Exemplary of the accepted stereotype are the White characters in Alexey Tolstoy's *Gadyuka* (*The Viper*) and Boris Romashov's play "Konets Krivorylska" ("The End of Krivorylsk"). In *The Viper* the Whites murder local citizens for suspected complicity with the Reds, abuse hospital patients, and exploit the people during the time they control the area. In Romashov's satirical melodrama, Sevostyanov, a former White officer, continues to indulge in speculation and sabotage as he tries to make his way in Soviet society. It is typical that Sevostyanov is in league with foreign interests attempting to undermine the Soviet Union. One may generalize that the standard Soviet villain from the end of the Civil War to approximately 1939 was a former White officer, or at least a White sympathizer, connected with a foreign government or capitalistic venture and eager to exploit or sabotage socialism for personal or political reasons.

The most active satirical campaign against the Whites was carried out in agitprop verse by Bedny and Mayakovsky. This activity paralleled the campaign waged by Averchenko against the Communists. Both camps exemplified the crude, distasteful, and personal. Bedny's propensity for phrase-making, personal vindictiveness toward the Whites, embodiment of the official stance, and agitprop approach to verse are evident in "Na Kubani" ("On the Banks of the Kuban"):

> There on the banks of the Kuban,
> Yes, on the Kuban,
> Such White trash,
> Nobility trash.
> The Trash pokes its nose into everything,
> Absolutely everything,
> It attaches itself, the scum, to the people,
> To the common people.
>
> . . . .
> The trash blabbers about God,
> The tsar and God. . . .[23]

Mensheviks, Kadets, Social Revolutionaries, the aristocracy, tsarist

officials, army officers, religious figures, and all other class enemies
were grouped under the general classification of White for satirical
purposes. The campaign was carried out largely in the official newspapers and magazines, which devoted considerable space to propaganda for the war effort.

Usually the works directed against individual Whites were somewhat more abusive than the more general treatments, although the
stereotype was more common. No White was more frequently or
bitterly exposed than Alexander Kerensky, head of the abortive Provisional Government. He symbolized all that was wrong with individual
Whites and their cause. The stereotyped attributes established during
War Communism were used by every literary faction to attack
Kerensky from its own point of view. In Kataev's *Erendorf Island*
Batist Linol, the Kerensky figure, is an insignificant lackey to Matapal,
the king of capitalists. When the office-palace is abandoned, Linol
surrounds himself with other lackeys and announces to an irate crowd
of workers that he has been chosen as the president of the Provisional
Government of Lackeys. He promises to work for the raising of tips to
75 percent and for limited rights for Negroes. In addition he guaran-
tees the two labor leaders (presumably representing Lenin and
Trotsky) all of their demands. He gives all the cabinet posts to fellow
lackeys but retains for himself the presidency and control of the Ministry of Finance: "Batist Linol was hardly the kind of man who would not
squeeze from his unexpected grandeur the maximum glory, lustre, and
dollars."[24] He meets frequently with bankers and billionaires and
boasts of his accomplishments:

> I have accomplished the great feat of liberating the people
> from the web of Matapal. . . . I have had smoking jackets made
> for all citizens! I have given the ladies bouquets of heliotrope and
> the children bananas! Finally, I have legislated the raising of
> tips. . . .[25]

Seeing much discontent remaining, he calls a Constituent Assembly
and names himself president but meekly leaves when the Lenin and
Trotsky figures tell him to.

Kataev's inept Batist Linol represents the accepted proregime
treatment of Kerensky. The only significant departure from the agitprop treatment was his emphasis on humor rather than invective.
Kataev's clichés were standard in exposing Kerensky: he was insignificant before the February Revolution and an opportunist thereafter; he

had no positive government program; he attempted to display magnanimity and to cultivate the support of the revolutionaries but was duped by Lenin and Trotsky; he surrounded himself with fellow bourgeois opportunists; his primary interests were power and money; he was proud and pretentious; he had monarchial ambitions; and he was a coward.

Typical of the Fellow Traveler image is Kiri-Kuki, in Bulgakov's "The Crimson Island"; his name phonetically suggests Kerensky. Kiri-Kuki's characteristics are essentially those of Batist Linol: Bulgakov emphasizes his pretentiousness, his currying favor with the revolutionaries, and his political opportunism. The use of allegory and fantasy by both Kataev and Bulgakov in the creation of an isolated island setting precludes the use of direct personal references and prevents the satire from becoming abusive. Bulgakov also places considerable humorous emphasis on Kiri-Kuki's human foibles, thereby temporarily removing Kerensky from the political light. Bulgakov was one of the very few to alter the context of portrayal, thus avoiding political attack.

Averchenko's satirical portraits of Kerensky are more splenetic; they express the views of the majority of the emigré community, which blamed Kerensky exclusively or in part for the failure of the February Revolution and the success of October. Averchenko himself blames Kerensky entirely, and the erstwhile head of state becomes the scapegoat for the Bolsheviks and their sins: the deprivation suffered during War Communism, the horrors perpetrated by the Communists, and the necessity of emigration. Averchenko uses the same stereotypes employed by Fellow Traveler, agitprop, and moderate proregime satirists, but he interjects a feeling of personal resentment and bitterness. In *Navozhdenie (The Inundation)* he condemns Kerensky as a bantering fool who comes under the spell of the Winter Palace's regal beauty:

> In the summer of 1917 there arrived from Germany in a sealed
> railroad car certain gracious gentlemen who took over the home
> of a ballerina, winked at each other, and pushed aside a verbose
> gentleman who was stupidly captivated by the charms of the
> Winter Palace; pushed him aside, and having gathered around
> themselves a couple of hundred socialistically-minded criminals,
> produced such a mess in the course of one year, that you couldn't
> untangle it in a hundred years.[26]

Kerensky's monarchial pretentions were a favorite target of all who exposed him, but Averchenko condemns him principally for welcoming back Lenin and Trotsky. Averchenko asserted that Kerensky's bombastic oratory, foolish resolutions, and political opportunism aided the Bolshevik cause.

Other frequent satirical targets were the White military leaders Alexander Kolchak, Anton Denikin, and Nikolay Yudenich, but none was treated so bitterly as was General Pyotr Nikolaevich Wrangel, who commanded the disorganized White Army after the defeat of General Denikin and who evacuated the troops from Sevastopol when the cause became hopeless. Proregime satirists singled out his inept leadership, his luxurious, bourgeois life, and his monarchial designs, and they treated him much the same way as most satirists treated Kerensky. Wrangel was usually portrayed as a foreigner and intruder:

> Ich fange an. I vill begin.
> Dis ist für all die Soviet place,
> Für Russian peoples in all die Land
> Der Baron's Manifest.
> Meine Name is familiar to you alle:
> Ich bin von Wrangel, Herr Baron.
> Ich bin der best, der mostest honest
> Kandidat für Tsarist Throne.[27]

Greed for Western money, a desire for power, and incessant defeats were the characteristics most frequently applied to these figures, who were castigated almost exclusively in the agitprop literature.

Linked with the White leaders was Marshal Josef Pilsudski, who was president of Poland during the Civil War. Mayakovsky frequently attacked him as an opportunist, a flatterer, a courtier of Western governments, and a pseudosocialist. Pilsudski's political stance was rather independent, and he thus became a natural target for agitprop satirists. Bedny's coarse approach is evident in this stanza:

> Pilsudski's almost Polish king.
> He has, though stupid as can be,
> The helm of power in pampered hands
> And leads to hell for all to see.[28]

As important a satirical target as the Whites were, the Entente nations and the political and military intervention they undertook into the Civil War received more focus. The satire appeared primarily in agitprop verse feuilletons by Bedny and Mayakovsky, but it also was seen in prose where the White villain was usually in league with representatives of one or more of the Entente nations. The original Triple Entente had consisted of Great Britain, France, and Russia united against the German Alliance, but when the Bolsheviks made a separate peace with Germany shortly after the Revolution, the Entente was shattered. Britain and France quickly turned anti-Bolshevik and spearheaded the intervention. The United States, a latecomer to the war, was lumped with Great Britain and France and was considered to be a de facto member of the Entente. The satire hurled at Russia's former allies can be explained by two considerations: retaliation for the criticism Russia received for making an early separate peace, thus breaking the Entente and allowing Germany to concentrate her manpower on the western front; and indignation at the politics of intervention into Russia's internal politics. Proregime satirists ridiculed the military ineptitude and bourgeois connections of the Entente, their national characteristics, and Western political leaders. Often mentioned in the same context was President Woodrow Wilson's League of Nations, which was attacked as bourgeois-dominated and in collusion with the Entente. Mayakovsky's "Chempionat vsemirnoy klassovoy borby" ("Championship Tournament of the World Class Struggle") treats the Entente and its political leaders in the accepted stereotypes of the day. The champions of each country are in a ring presided over by the referee Uncle Lazarenko, the socialist circus magnate:

> A crown, a large gold coin, and a sack labeled "The Profits from Imperialistic Massacres" are thrown into the ring. Lloyd-George struggles with Millerand over the sack, Wilson with the speculator [bourgeois Russia] over the gold, and Wrangel with the Polish gentleman [Pilsudski] over the crown. A red-haired Menshevik gets under foot of everyone.[29]

The champions all accuse each other of fighting unfairly and of biting. When the Revolution enters the ring, no one wants to fight, and the Entente asks for a ten-minute intermission. Typically for propaganda in general and Mayakovsky in particular, the positive resolution in favor of the Revolution exposes the weakness of the Entente.

The leaders of the Entente and other Western governments came under a constant stream of satirical abuse during the years of the Civil War and remained satirical targets throughout the decade. The principal targets were the British prime minister David Lloyd-George and the American president Woodrow Wilson, who were drawn as power-hungry imperialists and political buffoons eager to overthrow the Soviet Union. Both are attacked personally and as symbols of their respective countries, as are a number of other foes: the French premiers Georges Clemenceau and Raymond Poincaré, the American jurist and statesman Charles Evans Hughes, the British foreign secretary Lord George Curzon, the French premier and erstwhile socialist Alexandre Millerand, the Belgian socialist Emile Vandervelde, the Italian prime minister Benito Mussolini, the American secretary of state Frank Kellog, the Menshevik leader Yuly Martov, the French premier Aristide Briand, the British prime minister Winston Churchill, the French statesman René Coty, the Chinese general Chiang Kai-shek, the British prime minister Benjamin Disraeli, and numerous lesser luminaries. Though some of these men were politically less significant than Lloyd-George or Wilson, the treatment of them was no less abusive.

Mayakovsky's role in the treatment of the Whites and Entente nations was pivotal. Instrumental in creating the stereotypes of the White and Western political leaders, he did more than anyone to popularize them. He ridiculed these figures through the use of abusive personal references and an emphasis on counterrevolutionary bourgeois qualities. His own assertive and somewhat belligerent personality was very evident in these stereotypes, and he removed from them all notion of threat. By contrast the Communists in the works of Fellow Traveler and emigré satirists provoked a feeling of helpless fear. Mayakovsky's Whites and foreigners are just as brutal and unfeeling as those of Bedny, Leonov, and Romashov or as the stereotype of the Communist, but despite this they emerged as little more than harmless objects of ridicule, even during the uncertain days of the Civil War and the intervention. Mayakovsky's figures became accepted rather than the more formidable characters found generally in the works of moderate proregime writers.

THE COMMUNIST

The vast majority of satire touching upon the Communist dealt not with the famous individual but with the stereotype. The nameless and faceless Communist, who reflected generalizations about communism, was more often met than a historical figure. The satirical stereotype of the Communist was employed by all groups for their own ideological purposes. The emigrés and Fellow Travelers used the stereotype to apply the image to all Communists. Proregime satirists employed the satirical image to show departures from the norm of communism rather than from the norm of prerevolutionary life.

The initial satirical image was established early in the decade primarily by Boris Pilnyak and Yevgeny Zamyatin. Pilnyak in *The Naked Year* produced the caricature of the iron Communist, a ridiculous marionette whose slogan is "functioning energetically."[30] This functioning energy is usually encased in a black leather jacket and knee-length leather boots; the result is a dehumanized automaton. Essentially the same image is continued by Zamyatin in *Rasskaz o samom glavnom* (*A Tale of the Most Essential*) with the figure of Dorda. Zamyatin, however, rejects Pilnyak's emphasis on the ridiculous and transforms Dorda into a dangerous puppet. To achieve this he uses the recurrent image of a revolver:

> He took his revolver from its holster and was himself a revolver
> in a black, leather, or perhaps metallic holster, with loaded eyes.
> Placing cartridges into the clip, he says to his mother:
> "What, you went to church again? Eh, you old. . . !"[31]

As in Pilnyak's character there is an absence of human feeling and emotion and an intolerance for others. Dorda is little more than a personified weapon in his stereotyped leather encasement, and it was this caricature, more adaptable to melodramatic portrayals of brutality and abuse, that became the model, particularly for emigré satirists.

Bulgakov used this same tradition. In *Rokovye yaytsa* (*The Fatal Eggs*), after Professor Persikov discovers a mysterious ray which increases the rate of growth and the size of animals, he is confronted by Alexander Semyonovich Rokk, a Communist in charge of the collective farm "The Red Ray." Bulgakov uses semantically significant wordplay by linking Rokk with *rokovoy* (fatal), and the collective farm with the red ray Persikov has found. Rokk, dressed in the traditional leather jacket and boots, insists on having his way. Because of a national egg crisis Rokk wants to use the ray on chicken eggs at the farm. He comes armed with a plethora of official papers and documents from the Kremlin to requisition the machines (without being even remotely assured that the plan is feasible). Rokk's plan does prove "fatal" as the ray is applied to a misdirected shipment of laboratory snake eggs. Soon the country is overrun with monstrous serpents against which all of the efforts of the Kremlin bosses and Red Army prove futile. Only an

unexpected early August freeze saves the country. In the words of
Vyacheslav Zavalishin, "[The story] castigates the Bolsheviks' mania for
launching projects without regard for consequences and their practice
of hanging the blame on some scapegoat when the results were an
unpleasant surprise to themselves."[32] The scapegoat in this instance
turns out to be Persikov, who is attacked and killed by a frenzied mob
under the oblivious eyes of the police.

In *The Fatal Eggs* Bulgakov remains consistent with his original
interpretation of October and its ramifications. The result is more in
the mold of Pilnyak's caricature than of Zamyatin's. Dorda is a derivative of Zamyatin's initial view of October as expressed in *We,* and it is
expected that brutality should produce fear. Rokk is a product of
October viewed as a correctable mistake. The effects of Rokk's own
experiments are ultimately reversed and are portrayed in both a comical and horrifying light, just as October is in *Heart of a Dog.* In *Heart
of a Dog* after the dog Sharik has become Poligraf Poligrafovich
Sharikov, he mysteriously leaves for a time and then returns dressed in
a leather jacket and trousers and English leather boots. The transformation of the dog is complete, and Sharikov is the new Soviet man, the
Communist. He then becomes just as obtuse and dedicated as his
literary antecedents and immediately begins to purge the area of his
enemies, in this case, cats. The cats represent Mensheviks and all
other enemies of the Revolution as defined by the individual Communist. The Communist is given sanction by the Revolution to revenge
himself upon his personal enemies as his biases dictate.

The iron Communist did not remain as a fixed image throughout the
decade, and toward the end of NEP an expanded caricature emerged:

> Just as he was then ironically described as a "leathern man in a
> leather jacket" he is now mocked at as a machine-man, an adorer
> of technique and a bureaucrat who thinks that all moral problems
> will be solved by the progress of science, technology, and ad-
> ministrative measures. His personal life is swallowed up in his
> social activity: this activity, however, appears to be much less
> heroic than during the civil war and he is now shown as a cold
> automaton, a small cog in the great machine of the state.[33]

The revolver is now even further mechanized.

This greater intensity of caricature is found most successfully in Yury
Olesha's *Envy,* in which Andrey Babichev, a former revolutionary and
presumably iron Communist, has risen rapidly in the bureaucracy to

the ironic position of director of a communal kitchen. His life is immersed in becoming the epitome of the new Soviet man and in perfecting the sausage. Babichev is presented as so engrossed in the sausage that it almost comes alive, indeed becomes his bride, in order to belittle his total devotion to the administering and perfecting of the kitchen. In addition Babichev is caricatured physically (he is fleshy, resembling his own beloved sausage) and is frequently observed from a distorted perspective by the author's alter ego Kavalerov. The physical-external is emphasized to the extent that Babichev becomes a kind of mechanized animal. He exemplifies the direction in which the new Soviet man is going, and the insinuation is that a perfectly mechanized society peopled by automatons is the Soviet ideal. Volodya Makarov, Babichev's young protégé, and the symbol of the first post-revolutionary generation, expresses in a letter to Andrey his desire to become a human machine without a superfluous screw. The negative utopian elements implicit in such a view of the future link Olesha with Zamyatin.

Emigré satirists generally avoided the Babichev stereotype in favor of Zamyatin's dehumanized metallic weapon, whose absurd rigidity, devotion to trivia, and mechanization were sobered only by his motive of revenge. However, a note of bitterness and a more resentful tone are evident, and the vices of the Communist are increased. Emigré satirists emphasized unreasonable cruelty and abuse of power and tended to employ naturalistic detail and melodrama. The indictment of the Communist in Shmelyov's *Pro odnu starukhu* (*About an Old Woman*) is an example of this technique. Lenka Astapov, the Communist figure, is an extension of Zamyatin's Dorda. He plunders, kills, and confiscates in the name of the party and exemplifies the cruelty associated with this archetype. His cruelty and deliberate deprivation of necessities forces Pigachyova, the subject of the work, to go on a pilgrimage in search for food. On her return her train is stopped by Communist soldiers, carbon copies of Lenka, who conduct a search for grain. The animal and other nonhuman characteristics are typical of the stereotype:

> Just to look at them scares you. Red mugs, even green ones, all drawn thin! . . . their lips quiver, the most desperate sort you've ever seen. Then too, not everyone would even dare. . . . Such a collection,—only their eyes are human, and even the eyes are like those of a chained dog, furious! Their whole personality is changed, trimmed down. Well, you hadn't better talk, or it's into the cellar with you![34]

Averchenko employs essentially the same characteristics found in Shmelyov's work. Irrational brutality tending toward the tragically absurd, abuse of his privileged position, and exploitation are the dominant characteristics of Averchenko's portrayal of the Communist. In his treatment of the Communist stereotype, however, he is forced to avoid the personal references, such as he uses in the treatment of the historical forgers of the Revolution, and to return to the classical mode of satire by using generalized vices. His exposé remains ardent, but he resorts somewhat more to humor. These examples are better satire than his more invective works.

The stereotyped Communist is also found in the work of the rather independent Ilya Ehrenburg. After 1932 he became a Soviet writer who was quite securely in the good graces of the party; yet during War Communism and the early twenties he was abroad harboring significant misgivings about the ramifications of October. During these years he may be regarded ideologically as a writer between the Fellow Travelers and the proregime satirists. This vascillation is best evidenced in *Julio Jurenito*, in the chapter entitled "Veliky Inkvizitor vne legendy" ("The Grand Inquisitor Outside the Legend"), which has been omitted from editions of his collected works and most single editions of the novel itself with the exception of the original. In this chapter Julio takes Ehrenburg, who has been troubled by the famine, brutality, living conditions, and the continuing bohemian state of the arts, to see a noted Communist authority, who could easily represent Lenin or Trotsky but who is more likely the stereotyped Communist. The Communist has an incredibly narrow focus and can only assert that everything depends upon economics and should be subservient to it. The same monolithic approach to doctrine found in Zamyatin's "The Fires of St. Dominic" and *We* is evidenced by the Communist, who in sanctifying October comments that even if communism does not have the truth its followers must blindly believe that it does. The motif of enforced "salvation" is once again expressed, and although Ehrenburg uses Dostoevsky's myth of the Grand Inquisitor, who is willing to take the responsibility for giving the people bread and circuses at the expense of truth, the result is still the same. The Communist speaks in statements strikingly reminiscent of Vicar Dooley and D–503:

> We are leading mankind to a better future. Those, for whom
> this is disadvantageous, try to disrupt us any way they can: they
> shoot at us from behind bushes, they tear up roads, postpone the

desired halt in hostilities. We must eliminate them, killing one in order to save thousands. Others are balky, not understanding that their happiness is in the future. They fear the difficult transition and aim for the pathetic shadow of the past. We will herd them forward, herd them into paradise with metallic stripes. The deserter from the Red Army needs to be shot so that his children will recognize the full sweetness of the coming commune! . . .[35]

Ehrenburg's subsequent Communist characters are often negative and probably stem from his initial doubts about the new movement. Yet one senses that when Ehrenburg mocks the Communist, his pen is directed as much against the man as the system, while the Fellow Travelers concentrated on the system and the proregime writers on the man. In *The Racketeer*, Mishka Lykov, an egotist with a questionable moral outlook, becomes a party member after experiencing much confusion during the turbulent days of War Communism. He immediately assumes the stereotyped narrow and authoritarian approach to life initiated by Pilnyak's weapon and Zamyatin's Dorda. In this sense Ehrenburg is making a comment about the system, just as he is when he portrays Mishka's brother Artyom willingly losing himself in a sea of mechanical men serving the state. Yet when Mishka discovers that his ego can have no part in this new role and that he must become anonymous in a sea of devoted humanity, he rebels and leaves. It is evident that Mishka is the object of satirical jibes apart from his image as a Communist and that his actions while a Communist are partly the result of the literary stereotype and partly the result of his own character.

Ehrenburg also depicted, as did other authors of both camps, what may be termed the NEP Communist. Whether an old revolutionary or a Johnny-come-lately convert, this type of Communist willingly indulges in all of the vices of NEP but retains his position and privileges. In *The Racketeer*, Ivalov, who goes abroad with Mishka to watch over his political behavior, quickly succumbs to speculation. In Ehrenburg's *Burnaya zhizn Lazika Roytshvanetsa* (*The Stormy Life of Lazik Roytshvanets*), the commissars are the most active participants in speculation and the bourgeois life. The NEP Communist is closely linked with the satirical image of the bureaucrat that also emerged during NEP.

In contrast to the Fellow Traveler and emigré portrayal of the Communist, proregime satirists concentrated on exceptions to the

norm of the positive Communist. The exceptions were usually re-
formed or exterminated. A typical example is the figure of Budkevich in Romashov's play "The End of Krivorylsk." Budkevich is
selfish and abusive in interpersonal relationships and impersonally
devotes himself to a new power station under construction. He ultimately acknowledges his improper behavior but remains a failure
on the personal level. Romashov uses humor sparingly and seems
simply to have endowed Budkevich rather mechanically with negative traits as an example to others and then to have removed
them through an equally mechanical change of heart. Budkevich is
of much the same ilk as Andrey Babichev in *Envy* in his devotion
to construction and the system, but the difference in the resolutions of the two works demonstrates well the different attitudes
brought to bear on the problem by writers of the proregime and
antiregime camps.

Fyodor Gladkov's *Malenkaya trilogia* (*A Little Trilogy*) is exemplary
of the more proletarian proregime satirical treatment of the negative
Communist. The stories reflect the influence of Saltykov through the
use of predatory types, indictment and accusation, a lecturing tone,
and a social bent. The trilogy was written with the intent of exposing
harmful social elements, which could become part of the party, and the
stories are united through the figure of Mukhin, an old Bolshevik who
exposes the negative characters once they are in the party. In
Golovonogy chelovek (*The Cephalapodous Man*) Kovalyov, a climber,
plotter, opportunist, and careerist, is exposed. In *Neporochny chyort*
(*The Immaculate Devil*) the satiric barbs fall on Soska, a Communist
puritan, who sees dangerous deviation from the decreed norm
everywhere. (Soska even denounces a proposed toast to Lenin as a
bacchanalia.) In *Vdokhnovyonny gus* (*The Inspired Goose*) the object is
Budash, an oratorical windbag, who continually issues tirades in
agreement with the current party campaign and who is depicted quite
similarly to the Fellow Travelers' portrayal of Trotsky. The trilogy is
written in an uncaptivating style, didactic and devoid of humor. The
author's intent was simply to expose.

Those whom the Revolution brought to power were not always
Communists. Yet when they usurped control, they quickly assumed
the negative attributes of the Communist archetype. In Zamyatin's *A
Tale of the Most Essential*, Filimoshka has appointed himself chairman
in the village of Kelbuy because of a notice stating that the poorest
should hold that position.

And Filimoshka, chairman Filimon Yegorych, is no longer in his hut; he is in the miller's house, the one with Dutch stoves. He has all of Kelbuy right here in his fist, squeezing the very life out of it: for all of his knocked-out teeth, for all the holes in his clothes, for thirty hungry years, for everything at once.[36]

The ease and rapidity with which Filimoshka becomes a stereotyped Communist is another echo of Zamyatin's original interpretation of October. The difference between Filimoshka and the numbers in *We* is one of motivation. In *We* the numbers willingly surrender themselves to the United State because the power of the state has made them into machines by removing freedom and crushing individuality. Filimoshka, however, surrenders himself to the state in order to become an appendage of the state. He does this for revenge but when he does become part of the state he too becomes a machine. The revenge motive had been added to the stereotype by Bulgakov in *Heart of a Dog*, where it was linked with cruelty and abuse, evident in Sharikov's purging the city of cats. But Zamyatin uses revenge to focus on the power of October rather than on the pettiness of the individual bent on retaliation. In *A Tale of the Most Essential*, Zamyatin also indicates, as did Shmelyov in *The Sun of the Dead*, that the Revolution put into power derelicts who had neither the desire nor the ability to govern.

There were other motivations for accepting the new order besides the opportunity for revenge. In Zamyatin's *Ex* the deacon has made a public confession and announced in the newspaper that he is through with religion because of a speech he had heard on Marxism. He ironically enjoys the complete trust of the government even though he retains many of his old habits. Zamyatin, however, questions the deacon's motives: "But I know for sure: it was Marfism and not Marxism that produced a change in the deacon and prompted him to repent."[37] Ever since he saw Marfa swimming naked, he has become a devoted disciple of Marfism and appreciates the Revolution's doing away with the bourgeois concept of marriage, especially since his wife has caught him visiting Marfa. In the works of the Fellow Travelers, conversions to the new order are made usually from expediency rather than conviction, and the converts abandon few of their former attitudes and habits. The satirical stereotype of the Communist does not stem from these converts, however, but has its roots in the old revolutionaries who become mechanical slaves of the movement.

Closely linked to the satirical image of October and the stereotype of the Communist are the portraits of those individuals who were instru-

mental in bringing the Bolsheviks to power. The satire in these portraits becomes decidedly personal and pointed, and the accompanying
humor is rather low. Many of these works have the features of agitprop.
The emigrés produced the bulk of these portraits, and Averchenko was
the primary contributor. The figures of Lenin, Trotsky, Commissar of
Education Anatoly Lunacharsky, the founder of the Cheka Felix
Dzerzhinsky, and Maxim Gorky are treated by Averchenko much the
same as Western political leaders are treated in the works of
Mayakovsky and Bedny.

It is noteworthy that throughout Averchenko's work Trotsky and not
Lenin is portrayed as the leading political activist and the man in
charge of the Revolution. Lenin in fact is seldom mentioned apart from
his collaboration with Trotsky. In *Koroli u sebya doma (The Kings at
Home)* they are depicted as man and wife, but it is Trotsky who is
featured as the husband, the one who must go to the office to run the
government. Lenin as his wife has nothing more serious to say than
that "she" should have married Lunacharsky. They live in luxury and
always have plenty of food and fuel, while others starve in the streets
and burn their houses to get warm.

Averchenko does employ a great deal of humor in his treatment of
Trotsky. *Novaya russkaya skazka (A New Russian Fairy Tale)* is based
on the fairy tale *Little Red Riding Hood*. Singing the "International" on
the way to her grandmother's house Little Red Riding Hood gives a
foreign boy (Trotsky) her basket of goodies and blames its loss on the
wolf. The wolf, irritated at his undeserved infamous reputation, decides to question the boy. The question-answer sequence parodies the
original tale and at the same time humorously indicts Trotsky:

> Why do you have such a long tongue?
> The better to shout at meetings.
> Why do you have such a big nose?
> Why bring nationality into this?
> Why do you have such big hands?
> The better to open safes! You know our motto: rob the robbers!
> Why do you have such big feet?
> That's an idiotic question! How do you think I would escape to
> Switzerland after I get caught?![38]

Only after the wolf eats the boy and knocks off Red Riding Hood's red
hat (Kerensky's monarchial pretentions) is order in the forest (Russia)
restored.

Trotsky's penchant for oratory was frequently singled out and was depicted typically in *Khomut, natyagivaemy kleshchami* (*A Yoke Fastened with Pincers*), in which Averchenko attempts to convince a Muscovite of the necessity of going to hear Trotsky speak. The reaction is firm and negative:

> Listen . . . really, I already know what he will say. He'll call on us to endure another two years of privations, he'll enlist everybody to go fight on the Red front against the Polish Whites and Rumanian imperialists, he'll promise a world revolution for next week. . . . Why should I go, if I already know?[39]

The sameness of the rhetoric contrasted with the living conditions is a comment not only upon the men who utter long-winded orations but also upon the Revolution that has not lived up to its promises. After references are made to the Cheka, which arrests people for not attending meetings and not applauding, the citizen goes to the meeting. There he is given a policy statement by an armed guard (reminiscent of the Day of Unanimity in *We* on which the Benefactor and all of his policies are rubber-stamped) confirming all of his initial reluctance about going:

> We who are present at comrade Trotsky's meeting by an overwhelming majority endorse all Soviet policy, internal as well as external; besides that, we summon all Red comrades to the final Red battle with the Polish Whites; we express our willingness to endure as long as necessary all deprivations for the glory of the Third International, and hail also the Hungarian comrade Bela Kun. Hail to Trotsky, down with conciliators, everyone against the Poles! 1639 signatures follow![40]

Toward the end of the decade after Stalin had won the power struggle, Trotsky's rhetoric was more than hollow; it was counterrevolutionary, principally with its concept of the world revolution. Accordingly, at Stalin's behest and largely through the effort of Bedny, agitprop verse began to appear denouncing Trotsky in essentially the same vein that Averchenko had used before his death in 1925. Compared with Averchenko's sketches, however, Bedny's verse is more blatant and even less artistic.

While Kerensky, Trotsky, and Lenin were the principal satirical revolutionary personages during the decade, some of the lesser figures were also singled out, especially by Averchenko. In the collection

Dvenadtsat portretov (*Twelve Portraits*) he treats Nadezhda Krupskaya (Madame Lenin), Madame Trotsky, and Felix Dzerzhinsky. Madame Lenin is compared irreverently with the Emperor Caligula's horse. The emperor (here representing Lenin) so loved his horse that he made it a member of the senate, and because of the emperor's position the people and especially the senators were forced to honor the beast as an equal, if not a superior. Madame Trotsky is presented as a vain and frivolous woman with illusions of regal grandeur. She commissions her favorite, General Parsky, to build her a palace and discusses the great weight of the crown she must bear. Dzerzhinsky is shown rewarding children for spying on parents whom he subsequently executes. These secondary historical characters, included exclusively for ridicule, are treated personally and vindictively and are often used to criticize the Soviet system and the Revolution.

The satirical treatment of the Revolution, its extension, the Civil War, and those who participated in both, marks the most bitter and abusive phase of satire during the twenties. There appear to be two principal reasons for the temporary triumph of Juvenal. First, the apocalyptic and cataclysmic force of the Revolution provoked the deepest feelings of men to rise to the fore and created an irreparable rift. Second, in reacting to the new reality, satirists made extensive use of personal references and personal portraits that often sank beyond the splenetic to the crude and tasteless. The link between the new reality and the aggressive reaction to it was that in large measure the vehicle for this satire was agitprop works encouraged by the government and published by ROSTA. Averchenko's work may be seen as a direct parallel to this movement and as a personal reaction to the work of Bedny and Mayakovsky. As a result the literary quality of the satire was often low, and writers were more concerned with the act rather than the method of accusation. The works of Bulgakov and Zamyatin in this area stand as exceptions to the rule and contain some of the best and most effective satire of the decade.

3. The Emigré

THE FINAL extension of the treatment of the Revolution and the Civil War was the portrayal of the emigré who left Russia, usually during War Communism, for economic and political reasons. The satirical emphasis was on the political aspect, inasmuch as most satirists who treated the theme of the emigrant were proregime. These satirists attributed the economic chaos to class enemies who remained in Russia following the Revolution. The image of these class enemies, the emigrés-in-spirit who thwarted the establishment of communism, was transferred to those who emigrated. The emigré was depicted as a class enemy driven from his cozy life of exploitation by the Revolution. Anyone who fought for the White cause or who had White sympathies was considered an emigré. The stereotype included the aristocrat, the tsarist government official, officers in the tsarist army, businessmen, merchants, religious figures, weak intellectuals, and many members of the intelligentsia. Satirists concentrated on the figure of the emigré and only secondarily belittled his motive for going abroad and his life there. Fellow Traveler, agitprop, and emigré writers themselves treated the theme to a far lesser extent. Overall, the major contributors to the satirical image of the emigré were Ehrenburg and especially Tolstoy, both of whom were abroad and had close contact with some of the many emigré factions. Their treatment of the emigré and life in emigration was instrumental in moving the two writers securely into the proregime camp, inasmuch as the theme was largely a political issue.

For many emigrants the journey to Paris, the most popular gathering place, began with a trip from southern Russia to Constantinople. The type of people who made this trip and the conditions that accompanied and awaited them are portrayed in Tolstoy's *The Adventures of Nevzorov, or Ibikus* and *Na ostrove Khalki (On the Isle of Khalki)*. Those who emigrated encompassed the spectrum of Soviet class enemies and satirical stereotypes. Nevzorov himself epitomizes the philistine and the embezzler who has aristocratic pretensions and desires. Most,

51

however, are representatives of upper social echelons still able to demand luxury and attention. For Tolstoy and others the White official, tsarist officer, social aristocrat, and pretentious philistine comprised the majority of emigrants. Satirists viewed the vulgar philistine, the Nepman, the priest, and the embezzler largely in terms of contemporary Soviet reality as a point of contrast. The White official and tsarist officer were usually portrayed abroad for political purposes, since the Revolution and the ultimate victory in the Civil War intimated their eradication on Russian soil. In comparison the Nepman and philistine were more bothersome and dangerous. Tolstoy showed that the onerous system of class privilege (which he himself ironically enjoyed upon his return to the Soviet Union) is retained by the emigrants and that not all class enemies are equal. This assertion suggests that prerevolutionary life style was transferred in toto to Western Europe, where it merged with existing bourgeois conditions. Tolstoy expressed the view of the proregime camp that the exodus was destined to fail for all but the aristocratic elite. He accomplished this through the use of the symbol of the skull of Ibikus, which represents the shadow of death over those who emigrated.

The aristocratic representative of the intelligentsia was a success in Western society and was able to survive the difficulties of emigration. Pretentious, socially conscious, ostentatiously intellectual, and frequently frivolous, he was in emigration the same person who had been exposed as a social evil in Russia. The prototype was Alexey Tishin in Ehrenburg's *Julio Jurenito*. He lives a debauched life as an impoverished noble and comically considers himself an important political exile. Tishin is a mystic at heart, worships Nikolay Berdyaev and Dmitry Merezhkovsky, and views the war in apocalyptic terms.[1] He alternately wants to suffer à la Dostoevsky and be a pacifistic vegetarian à la Lev Tolstoy, and he grievously laments that the cherry orchard (from Anton Chekhov's play of the same name) has been destroyed with the coming of the Revolution.

Tolstoy expanded the image of Tishin more extensively than any other satirist. His characters in *Emigranty* (*The Emigrés*), *Ibikus*, and *Engineer Garin's Hyperboloid* are extensions of Tishin. They continually drink (with the agitprop campaign against alcohol this trait frequently characterized class enemies), think and act superficially, and attempt to cultivate connections in bourgeois Western, particularly Parisian, society. They converse only on the traditionally fashionable subjects of the intelligentsia: metaphysics, Merezhkovsky, Rudolph

Steiner, Berdyaev, and the French utopian socialists, all ironically
outdated in the view of the proregime satirist.[2] In addition to the
obvious mystical bent of the emigrant, Tolstoy emphasized a
sycophantic praise of Western culture, institutions, and life at the
expense of that just abandoned. This trait traditionally indicated pretentiousness and in the Soviet era exposed the philistine. Employed in
this context, it links the praise to pretentiousness and indicates that the
aristocrat is simply an extension of the philistine. Most exemplary of
these traits were the emigré White generals, who were made to
symbolize not only exploitation and an unwillingness to serve the
masses but also the Civil War and the horror of War Communism. The
agitprop verse of Bedny and Mayakovsky also concentrated on this
stereotype.

Type characters other than the aristocrat among the emigrés were
infrequent. Tolstoy employed the low vulgar edition of the philistine in
"Bunt mashin" ("Mutiny of the Machines"), an adaptation of Karel
Čapek's "RUR," but this type was usually restricted to Soviet life
during NEP. Tolstoy also added the image of the weak protagonist who
is psychologically and emotionally crippled and who is a vulgar reduction of Dostoevsky's Underground Man. This type appears in such
works as *V Parizhe* (*In Paris*) and *Rukopis, naydennaya pod krovatyu*
(*A Manuscript Found under a Bed*). The reasons for the lack of other
type characters seem to be the insistence that the emigré was simply a
displaced class enemy and the preference for using types like the
Nepman in a contemporary Soviet setting. Tolstoy's adaptation of the
Underground Man is difficult to employ as a readily recognizable class
enemy, especially on a political level, and the strong element of
psychology is alien to satire, particularly as it emerged in Russia in the
twenties.

While most aristocrats flourished in high society, others were less
fortunate and shared the poverty of the petty bourgeois emigrant.
Proregime satirists utilized the acknowledged poverty and unemployment to portray the downfall of the lower class emigrant. They showed
women resorting to prostitution, isolated aristocrats forced to perform
menial tasks, and parasites unable or unwilling to search for work.
These satirists showed that the deprivation characteristic of War
Communism was carried abroad by those who fled, thereby illustrating
the claim that class enemies were responsible for the economic chaos.
Tolstoy was the principal contributor to this image, but even he was
unable to dismiss the emigrés' plight entirely with a satirical portrayal

or an attitude of political ascendancy. Generally, however, he used living conditions to demean the emigrant. Agitprop satirists such as Bedny in poems like "Zmeinoe gnezdo" ("A Nest of Vipers") used these conditions as reflections upon the individual emigré and as propaganda. Emigré satirists used this distressing picture to create a realistic milieu for their work. Don-Aminado and Teffi were particularly productive in depicting daily life and portrayed the panorama of emigré life with a good deal of irony and humor.

The emigré did not escape satirical barbs from fellow emigrés, although, certainly, most of the literature written by emigrés about themselves was sympathetic and rather sober. Nonsatirical emigré literature usually portrayed the emigrant as a displaced person who longed for his homeland. Averchenko's *Tragedia russkogo pisatelya* (*The Tragedy of a Russian Writer*) good-naturedly mocks the ultraserious presentation of such feelings. He depicts a Russian writer bidding an impassioned farewell to his native land as he leaves for Paris in order to escape the horrors of the Revolution. In Paris he quickly loses the ability to speak and write Russian and seldom thinks of his abandoned home. On one occasion, however, the strains of "God Save the Tsar" rekindle old memories, and he exclaims in ungrammatical Russian: " 'Oh, notre pauvre Russie!' he thought sadly. 'When je come chez moi, je will write something pour notre glorious maman Russie!' "[3]

Emigrés were able to examine themselves and see some of the faults (usually nonpolitical) for which they were ridiculed by proregime satirists. The tone of unmasking was quite different, however. Emigré satirists exposed such faults with humor accompanied by a hope for correction. Don-Aminado, humorously but with a note of frustration, mocked the factionalism that added zest but little else to emigré life. In the poem "No. 4711" the tomb of King Tutankhamen, the Egyptian pharaoh, is discovered, and a meeting is organized by the emigrés to discuss the event and its ramifications. All factions from the passive anarchists to the "liberal conservatives" and boy scouts demand to be heard. Due to the tirading, no agreement can be reached on anything, and the meeting is adjourned. Such intricacies of emigré life were drawn much the same as intricacies of Soviet life and were largely the province of the emigrés themselves.

Proregime satirists concentrated on politics. The political orientation of the emigré as exposed by the proregime satirist was strongly anti-Bolshevik and was most evident in anti-Soviet propaganda and in collusion with Soviet enemies. This political stance was attributed to the emigrant's firm allegiance either to the deposed monarchy or to some type of representative government. Despite the disturbing factionalism, the emigrant remained devoted to his political ideals and fervently anticipated the demise of the Bolsheviks. The various factions did agree on this goal but argued over how it was to be accomplished and what form of new government to institute. A favorite satirical target was the fanatical and haughty stubbornness with which the aristocratic emigrants clung to this conviction. They confidently assert in *The Adventures of Nevzorov, or Ibikus* that "The Bolsheviks are a nasty episode, a temporary nightmare."[4] In *The Emigrés* they form the "League for the Salvation of the Russian Empire" and willingly cooperate with Western anti-Soviet elements. Some emigrés such as Don-Aminado saw the senselessness of hope and mocked the groundless devotion in a humorous fashion in such poems as "Obedinenie madam de Kurdyukov" ("The Society of Madam de Kurdyukov") and "Chem noch temney" ("How the Night is Darker"), in which he notes the futile ferocity of ideological combat.

Proregime satirists exposed the emigrés' tendency to distort Soviet life in order to discredit it politically. Satirists indicated that the emigrés left Russia with strongly negative feelings about the Soviet regime and that these feelings developed abroad disproportionately to reality. Emigré characters in works of this nature are fanatically devoted to the deposed tsarist order, and they slander the Soviet system whenever possible. The first expression of this trait in longer works is found in *Julio Jurenito*. Alexey Tishin, a dreamer and second-rate intellectual, returns to Europe with the rest of Julio's disciples following the master's death. Tishin attempts to ingratiate himself with the emigré community but is shocked at their obvious distortion of Soviet life. The emigrés assert that cannibalism flourishes in the Soviet Union and that soup made of infants' fingers is common fare.

Olesha's "Spisok blagodeyany" ("A List of Blessings") is one of the most thoroughgoing mockeries of the emigré fabrication of reality. The play was probably written as a conciliatory gesture to the government and does not represent the Fellow Traveler viewpoint or treatment. It is quite typical of the proregime treatment because of the strong role assigned to emigré journalism, whose purpose abroad according to proregime satirists was almost exclusively anti-Soviet propaganda and distortion of reality. As was common, Olesha exposed the figure of the journalist or editor, in this case Tatarov, but perhaps dwelt more on him as an individual than was typical of most satirists, who were usually content to indicate the content of the newspaper and to employ a stereotyped class enemy as editor. Tatarov is examined in a political light and dreams only of the overthrow of the Soviets and of the institution of a repressive regime which would punish Bolshevik leaders. This portrayal is reminiscent of the Fellow Traveler depiction of those whom the Revolution brought to power (for example, Filimoshka in Zamyatin's *A Tale of the Most Essential*) and is based on the revenge motive. In an ideologically acceptable conclusion Tatarov's prevarication is exposed and thwarted. "A List of Blessings" is typical of the proregime approach in that it shows the frustration and ineptitude of emigré attempts at misinformation and espionage.

The treatment of emigré journalism was harsh, inasmuch as it was through the mass media that the bulk of anti-Soviet views were disseminated. This treatment parallels the Fellow Traveler and emigré depiction of the Soviet press with its agitprop bent. Proregime satirists mocked the distortion and sensationalism which characterized the emigré press. This distortion and sensationalism were unmasked as traits of the Western press in general, but their presence in the emigré and American press was more pronounced. Ehrenburg's *The Stormy Life of Lazik Roytshvanets* contains a typical portrayal. Lazik journeys to Paris, the principal center of emigré activity, where he meets Ignaty Blagoverov, editor of the emigré journal *The Russian Fire-Alarm*. Blagoverov, together with Milyukov and his journal, *Voice of Freedom*, roundly condemns everything Soviet and carries on a furious propaganda campaign.[5] Ironically, both Blagoverov and Milyukov are forced to deal regularly with the Bolsheviks on the black market because their journals are bankrupt. These financial difficulties partially explained the sensationalism in which the journals and newspapers indulged to increase circulation.

Ehrenburg depicts the factionalism and infighting among the journals attempting to discredit each other as much as to slander the Soviet Union. The journals and newspapers become a microcosm of emigré life through the emphasis on factionalism. To the satirist some of the reasons for the failure of emigré efforts to discredit or destroy the Soviet regime were egotism and personal interest. Class enemies were those who sought to impose their will on others for exploitative purposes, and satirists showed that even though the opportunity for exploitation had been greatly removed in emigration, egotism remained and created contention. Tolstoy reacts to the theme essentially the same way in such works as *The Emigrés* and *Chyornaya pyatnitsa* (*Black Friday*).

The emigré desire to disrupt and perhaps overthrow the Soviet regime led to collusion with Western bourgeois and political interests and with class enemies still inside the Soviet Union. This collusion usually provided the basis for the plot to exploit or sabotage the Soviet Union. Tolstoy used this adventure novel situation more than any other satirist in order to mock not only the emigrant but also the West. In *A Manuscript Found under a Bed* and *The Emigrés* he examines the oil conspiracy fostered by Sir Wilhelm Deterding and the English, which attempts to drain the Soviet Union of much-needed capital. *Engineer Garin's Hyperboloid* contains several instances of collusion. A White general presents one of several emigré plans to Rolling, the multibillionaire, for destroying the Soviet Union. Rolling's closest associates are emigrants who eagerly work against the Soviet Union for personal gain. Garin himself intends to destroy the world and then build a new one in which he will be the absolute ruler. He devises a system of workers, rulers, breeders, etc., and an operation that will make everyone satisfied with his place in a novel that strikingly recalls *We*. To accomplish his plan Garin emigrates and secures Rolling's financing. The novel proceeds beyond the stereotypes portrayed in *The Emigrés* and *A Manuscript Found under a Bed* to a more individual and extensive treatment of the individual emigré and his activities.

The emigrant was less important than most of the satirical targets. Class enemies for the most part were treated either in connection with the Civil War or NEP, and the emigrant was portrayed as the class enemy who had fled. Thus, the point of reference was Russia and the Revolution. The most important stereotype of the emigrant, the aristocrat, had roots in both NEP and the Civil War and was in effect a composite of stereotypes. His image was based on the pretentious White and included an admixture of the philistine and embezzler. Proregime satirists emphasized the figure of the emigrant rather than his life or dealings; by demonstrating that the emigré was a familiar class enemy, the satirist released a number of clichés about the emigrant's appearance, life style, and activities. It was, therefore, unnecessary to examine the stereotype in emigration as thoroughly as had been done in a Soviet setting. The unmasking was accomplished largely by association and recognition. This was necessitated by the difficulty of juxtaposing the emigrants to positive Communists in plausible situations in Western Europe. The satirist had to rely on ridicule and a mocking humor. Noteworthy in relation to the general theme was the insignificant role played by agitprop and, for the first time, Fellow Travelers. Fellow Traveler satirists had little interest in exposing class enemies or issues outside of the Soviet Union, while agitprop writers concentrated on immediate national issues.

4. Contemporary Life

After 1924–25 contemporary life replaced the Revolution as the most popular single theme in satirical writing. Contemporary life meant, for the most part, living conditions and the economic situation. Every major satirist touched upon these themes for his own ideological purposes. Common subjects included housing, food, fuel, the economically stimulated rise in crime, public services, and the quality and availability of consumer goods. Perhaps the most popular targets were the dire housing shortage and the poor condition of existing housing, and the resulting problems. Satirists and the populace in general were able to laugh at the frightful living conditions following the period of War Communism and saw a comic element in daily life that was absent in the Revolution.

Frequently the satirist used an extended situation comedy based on the housing shortage. Such works were strikingly similar in their treatment irrespective of their ideological origin. Kataev's play "Kvadratura kruga" ("Squaring the Circle") and Averchenko's *Sentimentalny roman* (*A Sentimental Novel*) are typical. Despite their different ideological stances and literary techniques, Averchenko, a militant emigré who tended toward agitprop, and Kataev, a moderate proregime satirist who based his technique on classical realism, treat their material essentially the same way. Both base their portrayal principally on the humor inherent in the crowded conditions, and outwardly they mock the situation good-naturedly. Kataev includes some bourgeois types and juxtaposes them to serious-minded socialists of the revolutionary generation, but despite the ideological implications the interaction of these characters serves mainly to provide humor. His theme is the humor inherent in having two sets of newlyweds share living quarters. Averchenko's situation comedy emphasizes the shortage more poignantly, because he places an absurd number of people in a single room. They even have to sleep in shifts.

But the story contains no Communist caricatures, and the author makes no antigovernment statements. Only the authorial intent differs in these works. Averchenko, like other emigrés, exposed the shortage as an indicator of Communist economic ineptitude and of the regressive effect of the Revolution. Kataev, like other moderate proregime satirists, among them Ilf and Petrov in *The Golden Calf*, recognized the problem and attempted to expose it, while at the same time provoking public amusement. Kataev does not attempt to attribute the shortage to counterrevolutionary elements, as was done by the radical faction of the proregime camp.

Zoshchenko used the theme of the housing shortage more than any other satirist, and his conclusions expressed the opinion of the majority of the Fellow Travelers. Using the theme of the dire shortage of housing as a point of departure, Zoshchenko emphasizes the many years required to find housing, the people's unwillingness to part with a dwelling despite its condition or their attitude toward roommates or spouses, the high cost of housing, and their readiness to pay exorbitant rates in order to have a place to live.

Perhaps the best work Zoshchenko wrote on the housing shortage was *Mnogo li cheloveku nuzhno* (*Does a Man Really Need Much*). The narrator, who continually understates conditions because of his naive simplicity, travels throughout the Soviet Union to evaluate the housing situation: "And in connection with that, the housing crisis seems to have begun to abate slightly. We did not see more than seventeen people in any one room." He refers to a friend who finds a dwelling in Leningrad after only two visits to the Housing Division. The friend is elated with the discovery: "And there wasn't much need of repair at all: put in some doors, put up the walls, oh yes, and extend the stairs up to this floor."[1] He must also repair the chimney because his lungs cannot tolerate the smoke. Zoshchenko's title is an allusion to Lev Tolstoy's *Mnogo li cheloveku zemli nuzhno?* (*Does a Man Really Need Much Land?*), a didactic tale about a peasant whose consuming desire for land results in his death. Tolstoy moralistically counters that all the land a man really needs is that sufficient to bury him. Zoshchenko makes ironic use of the same contrast: in contemporary Russia a man desires to have an apartment; but because of the drastic conditions, he really needs and should be glad to get only a roof over his head, even if the walls and the entrance to that roof leave something to be desired. That the narrator sees a significant improvement in the housing crisis on the basis of these data underscores the seriousness of the existing problem.

The extent to which people would go to obtain housing was exaggerated by Fellow Traveler and emigré satirists to emphasize the problem. Long lines of hopeful seekers besiege those who, because of a death, divorce, arrest, or some similar occurrence, have a vacancy. Marriage is the most frequently used wile. In Averchenko's *Ishchut komnatu* (*Searching for a Room*) the narrator has slept for three months on soap boxes and for a week under the counter of a shoe store and finally desperately places the following ad in the newspaper: "I agree to marry the landlord's daughter in exchange for a room. Her age doesn't matter, the price doesn't matter, nothing matters except a room! Send all offers of hand, heart, and room to this address!"[2] The schemes to obtain housing, the long searches, and impatient waiting usually prove futile, and people dream, cheat, and connive only to be disappointed. In *Pushkin*, Zoshchenko's hero finds a room after months of searching, but he is quickly evicted because Pushkin once stayed there and the site is to be made a monument. For Zoshchenko, Averchenko, and others, the system is to blame for this frustration and disappointment, but this conclusion must be gleaned from the humor and irony since it is nowhere stated explicitly. Kataev, Ilf, and Petrov used similar situations principally to create comedy, and their satire concerned the individual involved in a situation comedy. Generally the moderate proregime satirist remained on the level of inoffensive humor and did not depict the comic desperation that characterized the work of Fellow Traveler and emigré satirists.

Bulgakov approached the theme of the housing shortage differently, by showing that a number of people continue to live in luxury. In his works he illustrates the failure of the Revolution to produce change. The complicity of Soviet bureaucrats and officials permits some to live in regal fashion, and thus, for Bulgakov, the system is responsible. In *Heart of a Dog*, Professor Preobrazhensky has seven rooms to himself, while all of the other residents have had to accept additional dwellers into their single rooms. Because of wealthy and influential associates, he continues to live this way in direct defiance of the Housing Committee. In "Zoykina kvartira" ("Zoya's Apartment") Zoya has six rooms, while the other dwellers live in very cramped quarters. She is able to retain this arrangement by bribing the house manager and through the influence of Goose, an important bureaucrat who lives in eight rooms himself. Bulgakov proceeds beyond Zoshchenko's laughter through tears to a more overt indictment of the system by showing that the housing crisis is a function of Soviet neglect and abuse. Significantly, these two works were censored, while Zoshchenko, even though he was criticized, was published in large editions. It is evident that the unstated literary strictures of the party, which had attempted to provide limits to the satirical depiction of the Revolution and the Communist, were enforced later in the decade on the themes of contemporary reality.

Satirists used the figure of the local housing authority, the *upravdom* (house manager) or the *predsedatel domkoma* (president of the housing committee), to add an ideological note to the theme of the housing shortage. In *Sorvalos* (*It Fell Through*) Kataev uses the figure of von Rebenkov, a former tsarist official who functions as house manager, as a typical remnant of the past who abuses the system. He is the stereotype of the White transplanted from the period of War Communism, a type which was used as a ready-made villain throughout the decade. Von Rebenkov comically cites some problem cases under his jurisdiction:

> [F]or my part I must direct your attention to the appalling position of still other proletarians in our building. For example, comrade widow Epoletov-Gaolyansky, wife of the late national hero of the Japanese campaign, lives in terrible conditions. She has two little rooms on the first floor that haven't been repaired for two years. One of the doors squeaks. It's terrible! . . . There is no place to receive guests. Then there is the honorable Banknotis, who is unemployed. His room, to tell the truth, isn't bad, but it's on the fourth floor! Horrors! Terrible! Can you believe it, he can't even go to the labor exchange. The cursed staircase wears him out. He is short-winded, and besides that he's Greek. Take notice of that. One may say, he's a national minority. You should meet him halfway. I'm not saying anything about myself. I live in the devil knows what kind of conditions. Would you believe that there is no place to put the piano? The seamstress can't even turn around when she is measuring my wife for a dress.[3]

Predictably, von Rebenkov's charges are evicted in favor of proletarians, while he himself is moved into a barn. By exposing an individual villain who is obviously in the mold of the counterrevolutionary, Kataev transfers the emphasis from the problem of housing to ideology. The figure of the housing official gave the proregime satirist the opportunity to return to the ideologically advantageous technique of treating individual examples of abuse, while still retaining a humorous portrayal of the housing situation itself.

Anisim Zotikovich Portupeya in Bulgakov's "Zoya's Apartment" is, like von Rebenkov, a bourgeois nonparty member. Bulgakov exposes him but uses his character for a different ideological purpose. Portupeya makes his living by accepting bribes from Nepmen, philistines, and wealthy party officials who wish to retain or achieve a luxurious level of living. His chief source of income is the NEP Communist, who is used by Bulgakov to shift the ideological emphasis from Portupeya to the system. Portupeya, Zoya, Goose, and the other characters make it possible for Bulgakov to expose practically the whole social order and, therefore, the party and the Revolution by implication. Bulgakov employs a good deal of irony and humor but depicts contemporary life in a direct manner, thus making the point through the portrayal itself rather than by editorial comment. He does not indicate that the changes in contemporary life are reversible or that they are the whims of those who profess to control events, for they are not his primary concern. Rather, the disparity in Soviet life exposes the failure of the new system. Reversal is then imperative, since the social experiments, much as the new Soviet man in *Heart of a Dog*, do not live up to expectations. One might well expect the government to abandon the experiments with housing officials and others and either to return to the status quo as had Professor Preobrazhensky or to try a different approach.

From the point of view of the common citizen the housing official was unresponsive and succeeded only in making a bad situation even worse. He was usually portrayed as either a hidden bourgeois or an unfeeling extension of the government. His appearance at a dwelling normally signaled one of two things: the rent was to be raised or lodgers were to be added. Frequently a bribe could forestall these events, and it is for this reason that Ostap Bender, picaresque hero of Ilf and Petrov's *The Golden Calf*, decides at the conclusion of his abortive pursuit of a Soviet millionaire that he will become a housing official. While willing to raise rent and add lodgers, the housing official ignored maintenance and repair, and several works showed public housing in a constant state of serious disrepair. The housing official was a secondary rather than a central character, but he was never portrayed positively; he was always made the brunt of barbs and jests and usually was little more than a personified comment upon the system. One must look into the nonsatirical and nonhumorous works of proregime writers to find a portrayal not dependent upon caricature.

The problems related to housing—food and fuel—were treated extensively by the Fellow Travelers and emigrés, who faulted the regime for the fact that many were starving and freezing. The desperation of the people and the aloof attitude of the party in dealing with the situation were cited frequently. The general lack of food and the quality of Soviet-produced and -distributed food were exposed in a sober, sometimes bitter tone. In Zamyatin's "Afrikansky gost" ("The African Guest") an ape brought into the Soviet Union dies in Odessa after eating Soviet bread. In Bulgakov's *Heart of a Dog,* Sharik comments on the marvelous food available at a bourgeois restaurant frequented by wealthy Communist bureaucrats and contrasts it with that from the state kitchens:

> . . .from the Soviet of Normal Diet. The things they do in that Normal Diet, it's more than a dog can comprehend. Why, those scoundrels make soup out of stinking corned beef, and the poor wretches don't know what they're eating. They come running, guzzle it down, lap it up.
> . . .Just think of it: a two-course meal for forty kopeks; but both these courses together aren't worth fifteen kopeks, because the manager has stolen the other twenty-five.
>
> What do you want with putrid horsemeat? You'll never get such poison as they sell you at the Moscow Agricultural Industries anywhere else.[4]

The regime preys upon the people not only by giving them rotten food through official outlets but also by making a profit from dire conditions. The quality of all Soviet goods and products came under satirical fire during the twenties, but nothing was treated more bitterly than food. Humor was used in the treatment of other products, but food was an increasingly serious matter.

Because the food problem was more acute in the cities, there was a great deal of foraging into the countryside, where grain was produced but frequently hoarded. Both hoarding and foraging were forbidden by the government in efforts to standardize food distribution, and at times to the satirist the Soviets seemed more intent on enforcing the ban on these activities than in supplying food to the populace. Enforcement and those who did the enforcing became the objects of satirical jibes.

Often the satirical treatment was bitter, as evidenced by the scenes in Shmelyov's *About an Old Woman* in which soldiers manhandle an old woman on a train and later confiscate her meager sack of grain in the village, thereby causing her death. The situation tightened to the extent that every person and every parcel coming from the country into the city was suspect. Zoshchenko's story *Doktor meditsiny (A Doctor of Medicine)*, in which a doctor returning from a collective farm is vigorously searched, mocks this excessive suspicion and vigilance. Unlike Shmelyov, Zoshchenko exposes these and other failings of the system in a humorous context. As serious as the problems were, the Russian people were able to laugh at most of them through the medium of Zoshchenko's satire.

The lack of money and the inflation that made the available money almost worthless were the most prominent economic subjects of Fellow Traveler and emigré satire. Zoshchenko wrote extensively of the lack of money and depicted a number of average people enduring embarrassing moments because of their poverty. The hero of *Aristokratka (The Lady Aristocrat)* almost assaults the lady he has taken to the theater when he fears she is eating more cream puffs than he can pay for. The host in *Khozraschyot (Self-Sufficiency)* drives all of his guests away when he begins to realize the cost of the party he is giving.

Aware of the pressing fiscal crisis, the government attempted widespread economy measures. These attempts, largely ineffective, were exposed principally by Zoshchenko. In *Rezhim ekonomii (The Regime of Economy)* the decision must be made whether to pay the bookkeeper or heat the toilet; the bookkeeper wins, but the plumbing freezes and bursts and will have to be replaced. Zoshchenko exposes such failings from the same point of view as does Bulgakov in *The Fatal Eggs*. Economy for its sake alone, without consideration for people, is reminiscent of the Communists' poorly conceived and ill-prepared project to curb the egg crisis with the red ray.

The theme of inflation was treated with a good deal more humor than was the lack of money, and hyperbole was common in discussions of skyrocketing prices. In Averchenko's *Characteristics of the Life of the Worker Panteley Grymzin*, 2,700 rubles are worth no more than two and one-half had been in the time of the tsar. In such works astonishing rates of inflation were considered to be a function of the government's mismanagement of economic affairs. Proregime satirists used inflation for humor, since it was difficult to obtain ideological advantage by attributing rising prices to a class enemy.

Even when money was available, however, Soviet products were either unavailable or, if available, were of poor quality. The unavailability of consumer products was perhaps more onerous than their poor quality. In Zoshchenko's *Melochi zhizni* (*The Trifles of Life*) the narrator saves for a year to replace a lampshade, but after searching all of the stores, he is unable to locate one. In such stories themes of the lack of money and inflation are combined with the unavailability and poor quality of goods to present a picture of general economic disruption. The lack of consumer goods was also lampooned by Bulgakov. When the author is offered a reward for having solved the mystery of Chichikov in *The Adventures of Chichikov*, he ponders the items that he really wants—a pair of pants, a pound of sugar, a lamp—but ultimately requests the works of Gogol to help him endure Soviet reality.

The poor quality of Soviet consumer goods became a standing joke among nonparty satirists. The laughter was loud, but there was a sound of frustration, particularly from Zoshchenko. In such works as *The Trifles of Life*, *Zelyonaya produktsia* (*Green Production*), and *Gotov letom sani* (*Ready Your Sleigh in the Summer*) Zoshchenko portrays the frustration of using worthless Soviet products. Because of the poor quality of Soviet merchandise, foreign goods assumed a special aura. Proregime satirists attacked the increasing interest in foreign goods as a trait typical of the philistine and the Nepman. The Fellow Travelers used the theme to underscore overall economic deficiencies. *Kachestvo produktsii* (*The Quality of Production*) is a good example of the satirical treatment of this theme. In the story a German has been staying with the Gusevs and leaves a pile of worn odds and ends when he leaves. The Gusevs pounce upon these articles and proudly display them to their envious friends as authentic foreign goods. A container of powder is among the articles, and Gusev decides to use it for talc. He is finally informed that the talc is really flea powder, but he undauntedly asserts that the discovery merely demonstrates the high quality of German products, because flea powder can also successfully be used as talc.

The satirical targets were by no means all economic. Many other everyday elements made living difficult at times, and these were singled out by all literary factions but primarily by the Fellow Travelers. The significant increase in crime was one of the most frequently exposed situations, and in satirical works crime became an accepted part of daily life. Almost everyone was guilty of some infraction of Soviet law. In Fellow Traveler satire Communist and non-Communist, rich and poor, important and insignificant all indulge in crime, and the universality of the problem reflects the government's own participation in crime and its inability to enforce regulations.

Two main aspects of crime were emphasized—theft and hooliganism. Anything and everything was stolen by almost everyone. The widespread theft, almost all of it petty, was attributed to markedly different causes by the two literary camps. The proregime satirist limited theft to class enemies and generally non-Communist types. The Fellow Travelers emphasized the universality of theft and often attributed it to the general economic situation and living conditions. The fact that most thefts were petty and that frequently useless articles were stolen indicated desperation rather than base criminal intent. In several works the articles stolen were the necessities of life such as food and fuel, and just as often theft was used to obtain a living: in Zoshchenko's *Drova* (*Firewood*) fuel is stolen, and in *Sobachy sluchay* (*The Canine Affair*) a man makes a living by stealing dogs for a crackpot's experiments.

Hooliganism was made the object of a concerted agitprop campaign during the decade, primarily through the work of Mayakovsky. Hooliganism was denounced as non- and anti-Communist, and ideology was viewed as the panacea. The Fellow Travelers also satirized the violence and rowdiness connected with hooliganism but added to it a mockery of the oversimplified Communist cure. Zoshchenko's exaggerated treatment of violence in the streets effectively exposed the problem of the average citizen and public safety. In the story *Draka* (*Fighting*) the narrator comments that life is normally quite tranquil around his dacha, but then he elaborates on the subject in typical understatement:

> Of course this tranquility doesn't last the whole month. Some days of the week just exclude themselves. Well, let's say, clearly—Saturday, Sunday, well, Monday. I guess Tuesday too. And of course holidays. Then too, paydays. On these days, it can be said, it's not good to go out on the street. Your ears ring from shouts and other sundry things.[5]

Though not as critical as crime and public safety, the topic of public services received more attention, and from the point of view of the satirist it was even more productive because of the greater possibility for humor. The humor was primarily that of situation comedy and anecdote and is best expressed in the work of Zoshchenko. The most frequent targets of satire among the public services were the baths and transportation. Railroads and trolleys were at best unpredictable under tsarist bureaucracy, but under the new Soviet regime they became one of the standard proofs of Shulgin's formula. All modes of public transportation ran irregularly; they were slow and usually filthy. Mayakovsky in "Banya" ("The Bathhouse") critically addressed the situation through the satirical caricature of the bureaucrat Pobedonosikov, who is writing a flowery speech praising the advances made in Soviet streetcars. In reality, according to the author, the prices doubled and only the color was changed. For the most part the agitprop faction preferred to expose national and international class enemies rather than to acknowledge domestic problems. When satirists such as Mayakovsky did approach domestic issues, they invariably included a negative non-Communist stereotype, who is either blamed for the condition or who attempts to conceal it for personal gain.

The public baths were portrayed as a disgrace and a scourge upon the people. Zoshchenko's *Banya (The Bathhouse)* is one of the most successful short satirical works of the decade, and the themes of the economy and poor living conditions, the comical frustrations of the average citizen, and a satirical picture of the public baths are mixed to create a microcosm of Soviet life. The narrator comically praises American baths for providing what are in reality only the basic services and then juxtaposes a picture of Russian baths, in which one is hardly able to wash. He laments that the clothing checks, one for underwear and one for outer clothing, are a problem because a naked man has no place to put them. He ties one to each leg and then begins a search for an unused bucket, which he locates after about an hour. There is no place to sit, so he must wash while standing. There is a virtual laundry in the bath, where people are washing a large variety of items, and this situation combined with the deafening din prompts him to leave. One check produces someone else's pants (his own had a hole in a different place), but the attendants will not let him exchange them. When he goes for his coat, he discovers that he needs the other check, but after undressing, he finds that it has washed away. The attendant wants him to wait until everyone is gone, but he describes the coat (one pocket torn, another missing, one button remaining) and receives it. When he remembers that he forgot his soap, he is reminded that he would have to undress to get it. Unable to bring himself to endure any more, this Soviet little man leaves. The farcical chain of events endured by the narrator in what the author refers to as a typical Russian bath and the prominent note of poverty effectively convey the point. In 1935 Zoshchenko wrote a sequel, *Banya i lyudi* (*Baths and People*), in which he alluded to his earlier story and through which he demonstrated that no productive changes had occurred.

The satirical portrayal of the Soviet economy and the living conditions of the average citizen was dominated by Zoshchenko. Only in agitprop, where Mayakovsky was the prevalent voice, did another satirist so master a given set of themes. Zoshchenko's preeminence is indicative of the fact that the satirical treatment of these themes was the province principally of the Fellow Travelers. The emigrés continued to concentrate on the Revolution and the Communist, and they treated the themes of War Communism far more than they did those of NEP. In the proregime camp the agitprop faction largely ignored the matter; Kataev was the primary spokesman for the moderate faction, concentrating principally on the economic issues themselves, emphasizing humor, and normally not attempting to affix blame. When guilt was a factor, he resorted to the stereotyped villains formulated during War Communism. Zoshchenko and Fellow Travelers also emphasized humor but added strong subtextual elements of pathos and desperation. They also typically used a combination of themes to convey more effectively an impression of economic chaos and deprivation. Guilt was a critical issue for the Fellow Travelers, but the government was usually blamed through implication rather than overt means. Bulgakov was more obvious than Zoshchenko and was compelled to accept the consequences.

The Intricacies of Soviet Life

While the economic aspects of contemporary life were the most overt indicators of extensive problems, the portrayal of other issues and situations dealt with daily by Soviet citizens gave depth and breadth to the satirical portrait of the new order by both major literary camps. While some troubles could be traced to tsarist times, thereby indicating a lack of substantial change, others were attributed directly to the Soviet takeover, principally in the Fellow Travelers' works. The tone adopted by both the Fellow Travelers and proregime writers was usually light and humorous. An exception was Mayakovsky, who scornfully mocked all deviations from socialist behavior and Communist principles.

A frequent target was the official penchant for renaming the streets, buildings, and almost everything imaginable after revolutionary thinkers and stalwarts of the Revolution. Both major camps exposed the practice. In works such as Mayakovsky's "Uzhasayushchaya familyarnost" ("A Horrifying Familiarity") the agitprop faction exposed the situation as a tiresome abuse of a revolutionary principle. Moderate proregime satirists portrayed the resultant confusion, and, as they had done in the economic sphere, treated isolated incidents as humorous anecdotes. Ilf and Petrov's *The Twelve Chairs* shows that even the cabbies become confused as the streets and squares rapidly change names. The Fellow Travelers, much like the moderate proregime writers, portrayed the absurd rapidity and thoroughness of the renaming and emphasized the confusion and chaos of the practice. Zoshchenko's *Parokhod* (*The Steamer*), in which the name of the ship is changed three times on a single voyage, is typical of the hyperbolic treatment. The difference in portrayal found in moderate proregime and Fellow Traveler works is one of intensity rather than substance.

The striving for significance and relevance in names extended beyond mere objects to people. Progressive couples began to name their children after revolutionary figures and to contrive names from Soviet abbreviations or from the initials of Soviet programs and institutions. This predilection for name changing was primarily a carry-over of revolutionary fervor from the period of War Communism, and the practice and its satirical treatment were confined essentially to the twenties.

In addition to the new names, the new Soviet vocabulary and slang were lampooned by the Fellow Travelers and emigrés. In Averchenko's *Sovetsky uchitel* (*A Soviet Teacher*) Vasya Usov is a teacher of the prerevolutionary mold who is having a terrible experience with the new Soviet jargon and abbreviations. His final test of overcoming the obstacle goes badly when he is unable to explain the meaning of the terms he is forced to use:

> Hmm . . . cough, cough . . . These same . . ."Derkombedy" relate to the "Uezemelkom" like a lower dependent organ, but in the event of misunderstanding all questions go to the "Gubsovnarkhoz," which is combined with "Osotop" and "Vseobuch."[6]

Proregime satirists also used the theme, but they attributed the lack of understanding to bourgeois individuals rather than the new vocabulary.

The change from weddings to a simple civil registration was also satirized. Marriage and divorce became as simple as filling out a form in one of the civil service agencies. This somewhat casual joining and rending produced a large number of marriages and divorces, as people did both for convenience. Marriages were often of short duration and were entered into for economic betterment or to secure housing. Survivors from the old order found the new concept of marriage confusing. This confusion and the difficulty in adapting to the new system were exposed by proregime satirists in such works as Kataev's "Million terzany" ("A Thousand Torments") to show the great discrepancies between the old exploitative order and the new progressive regime. Fellow Traveler satirists, in works such as Zoshchenko's *Koza* (*The Goat*), *Svadba* (*The Wedding*), and *Ne nado spekulirovat* (*Don't Speculate*), concentrated on the concept of registration and humorously exposed marriages of convenience.

During NEP the theater became one of the centers of a flourishing new social life. A new pretentiousness that was evident primarily in the satirical depiction of the Nepman and philistine was commonly linked with the theater, which assumed the guise of real culture and civilization. The philistine attended the theater to cultivate involvement with high society, while the poor attended, even though money was scarce, simply to enjoy for a change what they considered real life. This situation proved to be rich in satirical possibilities. Only those who had companions they wanted to impress or who had some other reason for pretentiousness stood in line to purchase tickets. All others—rich and poor, bureaucrat and copy clerk, party official and Nepman—besieged the theater manager for complimentary tickets. Significantly, the manager had none to give unless the soliciter was an important bureaucrat or party official. This obvious attempt to curry favor in high places was exposed particularly by Bulgakov, who treated the subject from the time he entered the theater until his death, from "The Crimson Island" through *Teatralny roman* (*A Theatrical Novel*, also translated as *Black Snow*) to *The Master and Margarita*.

All these intricacies seemed insignificant when compared with the mountains of red tape and the bureaucratic jungle of petty officialdom that could make every day a nightmare for the average citizen. Fellow Traveler satirists insisted that the bureaucratic monstrosity of tsardom had merely been taken over rather than streamlined or improved in any way by the Bolsheviks. They asserted that the Communists had succeeded only in adding still more encumbering details to a system that had been almost inoperative. One of the most onerous aspects of the system was the absolute necessity of having the proper documents. In all pious seriousness Shvonder, the chairman of the housing committee in Bulgakov's *Heart of a Dog*, comments that "A document is the most important thing in the world" (p. 99). Documents—identification cards, passports, food cards, trade cards, and other authentications—were portrayed as the rails on which the bureaucracy lumbered along. A pompous eulogy to the sanctity of paper and documents was pronounced by the comic bureaucrat Ivan Fedotovich Shmakov in Andrey Platonov's satirical masterpiece *Gorod Gradov* (*Gradov City*). Sent to straighten out the provincial city of Gradov, Shmakov views paper as the magic potion:

> No! We must have man become sanctified and moral since otherwise there is nowhere for him to go. Documents must be everywhere together with the appropriate general order of things.
> Paper is only a symbol of life, but it is also the shadow of truth, and not merely the ignorant invention of some civil servant.
> Papers accounted for on their merits and properly formulated are the product of the most advanced civilization. They instruct this depraved race of man and see that man's actions are in the interest of society.
> Besides that, papers stimulate people to social morality, because nothing can be hidden from the official office.[7]

The Fellow Travelers and the emigrés painted a humorous yet grim picture of the encumbering red tape of petty officialdom. Zoshchenko and Averchenko made the most extensive use of the theme. The horrors due to paperwork alone included the great number of authenticating documents that were everywhere necessary and the magic pass needed to enter an agency and proceed beyond the receptionist. The insistence that all activity be channeled through the official agency or functionary was compounded by the inability of petty officials to function even in the most minute and trivial areas without documented authorization. The overall ineptitude of the system was exacerbated by the ultracompartmentalization of the various agencies, which resulted in interagency ignorance and isolation from the public. The lethargy of the system was exemplified by the constant absence of the department head or his inability to see anyone and the unwillingness of clerks and petty officials to expedite matters in any way, thereby causing petitioners to wait for months as cases and litigations endured for years.

It was evident to the satirist that the situation was the result of unwillingness to cooperate rather than any lack of time or resources, and the encumbering red tape had become a way of life. These were the same complaints made by nineteenth-century writers about tsarist officialdom.[8] The distinctive narrowness of approach, characteristic of the Communist throughout the decade, from the weapon through the bureaucrat, was added to the uncooperative attitude and inefficiency of the nineteenth-century petty official to produce the stereotype. This enabled Fellow Traveler and emigré satirists to strengthen their original assertions that no substantive change had occurred because of the Revolution and that the automatons produced by October had a regressive effect on society.

Both camps and all factions exposed the red tape according to their own ideological bias. Zoshchenko's *Volokita* (*Red Tape*), *Galosha* (*The Galosh*), and *Naschyot etiki* (*Concerning Ethics*), Averchenko's *Zhivopis* (*The Painting*), Ilf and Petrov's *Svetlaya lichnost* (*A Pure Soul*), and Mayakovsky's "Bumazhnye uzhasy" ("The Horrors of Paper") feature the same opposing contentions of universality versus individual abuse and of condemnation versus support of the system. The proregime treatment, particularly the agitprop variety, can be construed as a campaign for efficiency. Bulgakov's *The Adventures of Chichikov* perhaps best shows the Fellow Traveler position. After establishing himself in Moscow, Chichikov fills out an extensive questionnaire prior to gaining employment:

> "Well," he thought, "now they'll read this and see what a gem I really am, and . . ."
> And absolutely nothing happened.
> In the first place, no one read the questionnaire. In the second place, it fell into the hands of a young lady clerk who did the usual thing with it: she treated it as an outgoing document instead of an incoming one and then promptly stuffed it somewhere, so that the questionnaire vanished into thin air.
> Chichikov grinned and started work.[9]

When the document is later needed, it is found only with considerable difficulty, and its absence contributes in no small way to the mystery of Chichikov.

While the emphasis was on officialdom's inefficiency, there was another aspect of the issue. In *Administrativny vostorg* (*Administrative Zeal*), a story reminiscent of Chekhov's *Unter Prishibeev* (*Officer Prishibeev*), Zoshchenko depicts the other extreme, the overzealous civil servant. Drozhkin, a policeman, and his wife are enjoying a stroll when the sight of a pig on the street makes him irate. He threatens to shoot the animal and arrest the owner, a helpless old woman. When his wife intervenes, he has her arrested. Through the character of Drozhkin, Zoshchenko extends the image of the narrow machine-man, formulated early in the decade, to the civil service to show the widespread results of the Revolution and the new regime. The application of the machine-man stereotype to petty officialdom was rare but marked a stage in the development toward the bureaucrat.

An aspect of Soviet life that was sometimes encumbered by red tape was gaining employment in the face of mass unemployment. Gaining employment was difficult because of the pervasive use of personal connections, which flourished during the twenties. It was a popular conception that employment was practically impossible to obtain unless one had an inside contact, usually a relative. Such nepotism came to be a popular theme of writers in both camps. The proregime camp generally treated both the benefactor and the recipient of the position with scorn and showed the practice to be a damaging departure from revolutionary ideals. Fellow Travelers used more humor and indicated that such conditions were universal. A typical case is found in Ilf and Petrov's *A Pure Soul*, in which hiring by connection ceases only when an employee becomes invisible, thereby making bureaucratic conspiracies and secrets impossible. The authors thus indicate that bureaucrats are more concerned with their own positions and ethical images than with providing cozy jobs for friends and relatives.

Once safely employed, the official attempted to improve his position. The variety of methods he used were the target of both camps. Ilf and Petrov exposed the briber in *Dovesok k bukve "shch"* (*Added Weight to the Letter "shch"*), Zoshchenko the flatterer in *Pautina* (*The Spider Web*), Averchenko the weatherman who tried to judge the political climate in order to be in tune with what was expedient in *Istoria bolezni Ivanova* (*The History of Ivanov's Illness*), and Mayakovsky the apple polisher in "Tovarishch Ivanov" ("Comrade Ivanov") and "Podliza" ("The Toady"). The primary differences in presentation among the factions were the scope of the problem (individual versus universal) and the use of more humor by the Fellow Travelers.

An intricacy of life affecting·those with positions was the fear of purges. Purges were mentioned often in satirical literature of the decade, particularly by suspect petty officials who continually dreaded the loss of their jobs. But purges in fact seldom occurred. Those expressing the greatest fear were those whose allegiance to communism was the most superficial or whose status in the party was most tenuous. The obvious way to avoid a purge was to ingratiate oneself with high party or bureaucratic officials or to broadcast one's firm devotion to the party and to the principles of communism. Both literary camps depicted satirically those who made such attempts, but the proregime satirists treated the theme more extensively in an effort to expose deviations from the norm. Ilf and Petrov added another tactic to the list of means of escape by showing in *The Golden Calf* several men in asylums feigning insanity in order to escape purges or to hide their bourgeois activity during NEP.

A method of protecting one's position and ingratiating oneself with the party was self-criticism, which became both chic and advantageous during the twenties. In *Chistaya vygoda* (*Pure Advantage*), Zoshchenko depicts Fedotov, a political barometer who is always in the vanguard of the current government program. When self-criticism comes into vogue, he makes a show of devoted capitulation. With this story Zoshchenko generalizes on party-prompted piety and shows that self-criticism was often based on ulterior motives. Mayakovsky condemned not the principle but the excesses and directed his assault mainly against negative Communist types. In "Kritika samokritiki" ("A Criticism of Self-Criticism") he attacks the fact that self-criticism had become a stylish mode and that bureaucrats and other false socialists practiced it only for effect. In "Novy tip" ("A New Type") he exposes a party member who constantly berates himself in the most brutal fashion, and the author expresses the need for real self-criticism rather than self-torture.

Both literary camps agreed that these intricacies of Soviet life include a number of heterogeneous conditions that made life confusing. Some, like renaming, were fashions to be expected after major events occur. Others evidenced significant social and political changes of emphasis, such as the replacement of religious ceremonies by civil registration for marriage. Still others exposed continuing social problems, such as the red tape of petty officialdom, which were only made worse by the new order. Whatever the condition the point of departure was a juxtaposition of old and new, examined for the most part during

NEP. The standard ideological viewpoints were brought to bear, but the light tone relegated them to a less important role than they had played during War Communism and in connection with the Revolution. The frustrated protagonist was frequently the traditional little man, principally because of the contributions of Zoshchenko, and the context was often a maze produced by a chain of confusing events.

The Embezzler

Embezzlement became a serious social problem in the twenties. The embezzler became the object of a feuilleton campaign, principally by proregime spokesmen, and later the subject of longer works of literature. Most satirists dealt with the problem, emphasizing its startling magnitude. The usual difference in emphasis between the two camps—universality versus individual abuse—did not exist for this issue. Both camps freely acknowledged the widespread nature of the problem, since there appeared to be no ideological advantage to be gained by narrowing the scope, but exposed the extent of embezzlement for markedly different reasons. Both factions of the proregime camp carried out what amounted to an agitprop campaign, emphasizing the seriousness of the problem in order to convey a note of urgency and make the propaganda more successful. In contrast the Fellow Travelers wanted to expose the inability of the government to cope with embezzlement and to show Communist participation in crime.

The most successful work to deal with this theme, Kataev's *The Embezzlers*, became one of the classics of Soviet satire.[10] Kataev indicates the universality of embezzlement on the initial page of the work:

> Embezzlers are running all over. It's obvious. They get into coaches with government money and ride off. But no one knows where they go. One must assume that they ride from city to city. For example, today I read a critique that indicates that in Moscow during October no less than 1500 people from various institutions left in this manner.[11]

The story shows that embezzling government money has become so common that people not only expect it but find methods of profiting from it. High-priced prostitutes and swindlers are able to make a comfortable living by preying upon the hordes of embezzlers, who are typically reckless with money they are unaccustomed to having. While much humor is employed, the conclusion features an abrupt change of tone, typical of many satirical works. Prokhorov, the erstwhile embezzler, returns to the capital to find his family totally destitute, freezing, and starving. He is sentenced and quickly sent to prison. The sudden seriousness underscores the moral and effectively exposes that which earlier had been treated only humorously.

Both literary camps exposed the act of embezzlement in quite similar terms, but the figure of the embezzler usually reflected the ideological biases of the particular group. In *The Embezzlers*, Prokhorov is an older remnant of the past, who has endured the war and the Revolution unscathed and unchanged. Mishka Lykov in Ehrenburg's *The Racketeer* is a younger figure from the prerevolutionary years, who acquired his criminal tendencies before October. In A. N. Tolstoy's *The Adventures of Nevzorov, or Ibikus* the embezzlers are emigrating Whites and White sympathizers, who also may be counted as remnants of the past. The Fellow Travelers in contrast did not insist that the embezzler come from the past, and even though they recognized that pre-October elements were likely to be involved in the crime wave they also cast bureaucrats, party officials, and other Soviet functionaries as embezzlers.

The Soviet villain is usually caught and punished. The embezzler was certainly no exception, even though many methods of escape or avoiding punishment were attempted. On the way back to Moscow, Prokhorov notices one of his fellow embezzlers diligently studying the criminal code looking for loopholes, while the characters in *Ibikus* emigrate and take all they can with them. In Zoshchenko's *Svyatochnaya istoria (A Christmas Tale)* the embezzler attempts to feign death in order to escape, while in other stories insanity is pretended. With the exception of emigration all of the attempts fail.

THE BUREAUCRAT

The figure of the Communist had developed from the weapon to the bureaucratic machine-man, most evident in the figure of Andrey Babichev in Yury Olesha's *Envy*. Once the transition had become complete, the bureaucrat became one of the favorite targets of the proregime satirists, who were to follow the simple guideline that the satirist should expose bureaucratic abuses rather than indict the party structure. The two general types of bureaucrats singled out within these strictures were the Andrey Babichev type used by the Fellow Travelers and the masked bourgeois, who appeared in the works of both major literary camps. The masked bourgeois was either the NEP Communist alluded to or the philistine. In the words of van der Eng-Liedmeier: "This tendency of exposing the bureaucrat as a hidden bourgeois in his private life, as an enemy of the future communist society, we also find in other communist authors, such as Gladkov, Semenov, and Libedinskij. . . . Unlike the . . . fellow-travellers they do not give a caricature of the bureaucratic type, they tear off his mask by giving a realistic description of his faults. Thus the 'iron communist' of the civil war may gradually change into a NEP-bureaucrat" (p. 28). Libedinsky's *Komissary* (*The Commissars*) with the figure of Rozov, Gladkov's *Tsement* (*Cement*) with the figure of Badin, and Semyonov's *Natalya Tarpova* with the figure of the factory party executive are all examples of the low-key exposé produced by pro-regime writers. Badin is a good example of the realistic, somewhat balanced portrayal, in that his sexual appetite and other interpersonal abuses are weighed against his ability as an administrator.

For the most part these works are rather sober and steeped in ideology and only remotely use the satirical mode. The satirical portrait of the NEP bureaucrat is most successfully conveyed in the work of Mayakovsky, Bulgakov, and Romashov. Mayakovsky's "The Bathhouse" stands as one of the outstanding satirical works of the decade and was written with the express purpose of exposing negative bureaucratic elements. The central target is Pobedonosikov, whose pre-October life is highly suspect. This circumstance gives Mayakovsky the opportunity to attribute Pobedonosikov's negative qualities to non-Soviet factors. His character is replete with stereotyped faults. His speech praising the advances made in Soviet streetcars is a fabrication of the truth and an attempt to ingratiate himself with higher party officials. The speech also contains digressions on Pushkin and Tolstoy, thereby exposing him as an aspiring intellectual. He is seldom available in his office and takes no observable interest in the practical affairs of the department. His bourgeois tendencies manifest themselves in the purchase of expensive French furniture and the commissioning of his portrait in a heroic pose atop a white steed. He is not versed in Communist ideology. His opportunism is evident as he tries to undermine everyone else in an attempt to travel into the future with the Phosphoric Woman. His professed intellectualism and bourgeois tastes immediately label him as a Nepman, while other characteristics bear more directly upon his position in the bureaucracy. It is Pobedonosikov's abuse of his position that makes it possible for him to indulge in

the philistine life so repugnant to Mayakovsky. This abuse and in-
dulgence were the principal satirical attributes of the bureaucrat.

A similar stance is taken by Boris Romashov in his most accomplished play "Vozdushny pirog" ("The Meringue Pie"). The bureaucratic target is Ilya Koromyslov, a bank director, whose character
reflects the bureaucratic stereotype used by proregime writers. The
combination of bureaucratic abuse and plush living is essentially the
same as that depicted in "The Bathhouse," and Pobedonosikov and
Koromyslov emerge as blood brothers. The only difference is
Romashov's soberly punitive tone. Both characters are exposed in the
final act, and the authors demonstrate that such men are definitely
doomed to failure in Soviet society.

Mikhail Bulgakov in "Zoya's Apartment" makes no such admission.
The satirized bureaucrat is Goose, whose exorbitant salary and
privileged position ensure a luxurious life. Bulgakov mentions little
about his administrative activity save that Goose employs strategic
bribes and connections to his own advantage. The characteristic Bulgakov emphasizes through Goose is wealth and luxurious living, which
is closely linked with the theme of housing. This emphasis is used as
much to attack the Soviet system, which is quite willing to allow Goose
to function as he pleases, as it is to expose the figure of the bureaucrat.
Goose is portrayed as a more influential and powerful man than either
Pobedonosikov or Koromyslov and is never exposed by the author in a
direct verbal or dramatic manner. His demise comes not from the
forces of alternative good but from the knife of a Chinese robber. The
implication is that Goose could have continued functioning with the
blessing of the Soviets had he not met a sudden end.

Official bureaucratic activities were of as much interest to proregime
satirists as was the private life of the character. To many writers the
seemingly endless formation of commissions and their involvement
with trivia were little more than a distressing attempt at self-perpetua-
tion. In this sense the bureaucrat recalls the petty official. Bureaucratic
concern with trivia is ridiculed in Ehrenburg's *The Stormy Life of
Lazik Roytshvanets*, which utilizes the travel motif to expose various
elements of Soviet and Western European life. In Tula, Lazik is given
the responsibility of breeding pure-blooded rabbits, all of which
quickly die, thereby foiling the experiment. His supervisor instructs
him to ignore the setback and to proceed as if the rabbits were still
alive. A questionnaire arrives from Moscow; it reflects the bureaucratic
preoccupation with impractical and insignificant data:

What influence has the set-up of pure-blooded rabbit-breeding had (a) on the economic state of the peasants, (b) on their cultural life, and (c) on their family relationships? Is there any observable connection between this and the fertility rate? In round figures give the correlation between rabbit population and the soap demand as per peasant economy (p. 74).

Lazik's superior asks him to boast of their achievements in rabbit breeding and to illustrate them with many charts and tables. Accordingly he fabricates an elaborate report, only to be arrested when a special commission arrives to observe the successful techniques. His superior continues to function and is unaffected by the commission. Thus, the system is impervious to change or threat, while people suffer the consequences of bureaucratic inefficiency and abuse.

Andrey Platonov's *Gradov City* reflects a satirical orientation toward bureaucracy similar to that of *The Stormy Life of Lazik Roytshvanets* and is an excellent example of the moderate proregime approach to the issue. Bumbling bureaucrats naively perceive ideology as the solution to all problems, and in an attempt to modernize Gradov in the new Soviet era a commission is formed to find technicians for the proposed hydrotechnical projects: "But the commission did not accept a single technician, because it turned out that in order to build a village well the technician had to know all the teachings of Karl Marx." Undaunted by failure in small ventures the resident bureaucrats then attempt to have Gradov designated as a regional center and approach the problem by launching a massive effort to build a canal "for direct access into Gradov by Persian, Mesopotamian and other commercial ships."[12] This effort is supplemented by a four-hundred-page document on how to administer the proposed region with Gradov as its center and with extensive plans for air service. Moscow judiciously avoids naming Gradov a regional center, and Platonov is comfortably able to expose problems while showing the mature revolution in Moscow as the alternative. The bureaucratic thrust behind many of the schemes in the work, Ivan Shmakov, also considers such projects as putting all of the earth's water underground and having the sun always shine as a visible symbol of the administrative center. He also objects to nature as unplanned chaos and views the bureaucratic offices as a way to transform the elements into a world of order. Shmakov thus recalls Zamyatin's portrayal of the rigidity of the new order and its adherents and marks one of the few examinations of the machine-man by a proregime satirist. It is noteworthy that Shmakov dies after exhausting himself trying to write a book entitled *Principles of Depersonalizing Man with the Goal of Transforming Him into the Perfect Citizen with Lawfully Regulated Actions Every Minute of His Existence.*

The necessity of streamlining the bureaucracy and improving the performance of its major functionaries was obvious, but there was fear that bureaucratic abuses and methods, extant since tsarist times, were too deeply ingrained to permit reform. Kataev raised these issues in *Smertelnaya borba* (*A Life and Death Struggle*), in which a bureaucrat becomes so incensed at a newspaper article exposing the abuses of the bureaucracy that he decides to improve the situation. He assigns the task of drawing up a plan of attack to his assistant, but since his assistant is out of town, he functions as his own assistant. He sends himself memos, refuses to act expeditiously, argues with himself, sets up rigid guidelines and complex channels, and insists that others treat him as two people.

At the end of the decade the bureaucrat in satirical writing was a composite of two basic stereotypes, the machine-man and the masked bourgeois. Fellow Traveler satirists employed both about equally. They always portrayed the machine-man as a Communist and used his depersonalized existence as a wedge against the Revolution. The machine-man devoted his personal life to the system to the extent that his private life disappeared. The masked bourgeois in Fellow Traveler satire was usually not a Communist, even though it would have been advantageous to portray a bourgeois party member. It was just as serious an indictment to show a non-Communist bourgeois operating successfully within the Soviet system. The Fellow Traveler bureaucrat, irrespective of type, was more powerful than his proregime counterpart, and he was seldom punished. He was part of the new Soviet aristocracy, whether a Communist or not, and his position transcended the influence of revolutionary ideology. For the most part Fellow Travelers emphasized the bureaucrat's private life and gave little attention to his official functions. This emphasis satirized Communism by showing the mode of life still possible under it. Emigré satire did not treat the bureaucrat to any significant extent, and this theme remained a local issue.

Proregime satirists confined themselves largely to the masked bourgeois type but seldom made him a Communist. The personal life of the masked bourgeois was characterized by pretentiousness and regal living, while his official life exemplified a disinterest in administrative procedures and a desire to use his position for personal gain.

The proregime portrayal of the bureaucrat emphasized ineptitude and punishment. Bureaucrats schemed and plotted, but their activities were rendered harmless as they were juxtaposed to positive characters. A balanced portrayal of private and official life was used, and these two lives were fused into a bourgeois whole.

NEW ECONOMIC POLICY

The years of the New Economic Policy provided not only the targets for many of the satirical barbs dealing with contemporary life but also many of the finest examples of Soviet satire. It was during NEP that the embezzler and bureaucrat flourished. NEP also provided its own special targets. The ever present Russian philistine assumed a new tone and vigor, while the figure of the Nepman grew out of the combined images of the philistine and the petty bourgeois class enemy. These two archetypes became the central figures of much of the outstanding satire of the decade and the target of both major literary camps.

The outstanding contributor to the figure and activity of the philistine during the decade was Zoshchenko. His work best defines the Soviet version of the philistine: ignorant, poorly versed in the proper ideology, narrow-minded, greedy, prejudiced, preoccupied with trivia, smug, materialistic, and vulgar.

While Zoshchenko's short stories exposed the various characteristics of the philistine, the best portrayal in a single work is found in Mayakovsky's "Klop" ("The Bedbug"), which was written toward the end of the decade and which synthesized the established traits of the new philistine. Mayakovsky campaigned against philistinism all his life and quickly pointed out the emergence of the new philistine. In the play David Renaissance, his wife Rozalia, and Oleg Bayan, the ideologue of the philistine movement, are cast as traditional philistines of the prerevolutionary mold. Ivan Prisypkin, who talks in pseudorevolutionary phrases and casts himself in the role of the old revolutionary warrior, is the new Soviet philistine. He stems from traditional sources, as indicated by his ties with Bayan, but is nevertheless a product of the twenties. That both editions of the philistine are closely linked is shown in the symbolic marriage of Prisypkin to Elzevira Renaissance, David's daughter.

Prisypkin is the epitome of the stereotype of the philistine during the twenties. His lack of refinement shows in his personal appearance and dwelling, which indicate lack of attention and a tendency toward

swinishness, and he often uses vulgarities and coarse expressions. Yet
he has aristocratic pretentions, as evidenced by his changing his name
to the refined Pierre Skripkin (derived from *skripka*, violin) and by his
desire to give his children aristocratic names. His low nature is evidenced by the fact that Zoya Beryozkina is pregnant by him, and he
makes his living by giving lessons on how to dance, write verse, and
borrow money. His Western bourgeois tendencies manifest themselves in his interest in acquiring many possessions; he plays the guitar
and dances the fox trot, and he enjoys drinking and romancing. The
philistine, then, was linked with most of the satirically perceived vices
of the decade. These characteristics are often treated individually or a
few at a time by other satirists, but never was the saturation of caricature so prominent. Never one for subtle effects, Mayakovsky univer-
salized the image of Prisypkin in the famous concluding scene in which
the hero turns to the audience, recognizes people of his own ilk, and
appeals to them for help, insinuating that Prisypkins are rampant in
Soviet society.

Of all the stereotyped attributes the desire to be part of high society
and to be near to aristocrats was perhaps the most indispensable.
Together with this desire was found a pervasive pretentiousness that
often blinded the would-be aristocrat to reality. In Zoshchenko's
Madona (*The Madonna*) the narrator's craving for aristocratic company
to pamper his ego leads him to a beautiful woman clad in expensive
clothes and furs. His elaborate praise of her qualities, particularly her
aristocratic bearing, is dimmed only slightly by the ultimate realization
that she is simply an expensive prostitute. Alexey Tolstoy's emigré
Nevzorov in *The Adventures of Nevzorov, or Ibikus* and Kataev's
embezzler Prokhorov in *The Embezzlers* were also driven by similar
pretentiousness and reflect the extensive application of satire to the
philistine.

Next in importance for the philistine were money and consumer
goods, which frequently drove him to theft and conspiracy. Indeed,
the problem of embezzlement in the eyes of the satirist was attributable to the greed present in the philistine, and the figure of the embezzler was often indistinguishable from that of the philistine. Kataev in
Veshchi (*Things*), *Zimoy* (*Winter Time*), "Squaring the Circle," and *The
Embezzlers*, and Zoshchenko in *Klad* (*The Hoard*), *Silnee smerti*
(*Stronger than Death*), and *Monastyr* (*The Monastery*) were most
active in portraying avarice. Characteristic of their work were amusing
anecdotes about the worship of money. In *Winter Time* a poor poet falls

in love, but his path to marriage is blocked by his intended's brother, who expounds on the dollar in the most elaborate philistine rhetoric: "There you are. The dollar, my dear chap, is everything. I worship the dollar. I love the dollar. Five dollars equals one pound sterling. Just so. It is the unit of measuring man's right to exist."[13] In Bulgakov's "Beg" ("The Flight") Korzukhin echoes the same thought: "The dollar! That great omnipotent spirit!"[14] Korzukhin has emigrated to Paris, and that city, along with the United States, was considered the bastion of philistine thought and aspirations.

Praising things foreign and speaking foreign languages assumed a certain mystique for the philistine. This fact may be considered a result of the aristocratic pretentiousness that was so common, and the satirist applied the assumption of chic cosmopolitan airs to all but the most petty and vulgar. The foreign language is usually spoken with terrible pronunciation and grammar, and French is the language most frequently abused, undoubtedly because it had served so long as the language of culture and refinement.

This pretentiousness combined with a desire to ingratiate oneself into the new order resulted in much overblown rhetoric about pretended liberal and revolutionary activity that was ordinarily anathema to the conservative and narrow-minded philistine. Kataev's *Ekzemplyar (The Specimen)* is among the better examples of how the Soviet satirist approached the issue. The central figure is "the only one of its kind in the whole USSR, the rarest of its type, a specimen of the philistine of 1905."[15] *The Specimen* is reminiscent of "The Bedbug" in technique in that the philistine has been in a lethargic sleep since 1905 and is kept in a museum. Upon awakening and evaluating the situation, he takes full advantage of the opportunity to praise his revolutionary activity:

> 1905? Why, of course I remember! I might even say that I personally participated in the struggle against absolutism. I was even in prison, you know. For taking part in a demonstration. . . . Those were the days! What I couldn't tell you! . . . Ah yes, we old social revolutionaries! In general, we're an endangered species, you know. . . .[16]

Despite pretentions the philistine remained basically a coarse individual, and the satirist attempted to demonstrate this through speech and actions. Philistines use drugs, employ coarse vocabulary, and commit base acts. The drug theme is prominent in *The Adventures of*

Nevzorov, or Ibikus and "Zoya's Apartment," in which the Chinese Gan-Dza-Lin, comically called Gazolin, does a thriving trade in opium and other drugs with the customers and operators of Zoya's brothel. Drugs are infrequently mentioned in the literature of the decade and are essentially limited to the characterization of the philistine. Coarse behavior is personified in *Heart of a Dog* by Sharikov, who, though the new Soviet man, is not yet housebroken. Bulgakov indicates that the new Soviet man is simply the new edition of the old philistine.

The Nepman was essentially the philistine with emphasized bourgeois traits. Those traits that received the most satirical attention were dancing the fox-trot, the desire to acquire petty material possessions, and a capitalistic bent most evident in speculation. Geraniums, curtains, and canaries all became stereotypes of petty bourgeois possessions and symbolized the preoccupation with seemingly insignificant acquisitions. In Mayakovsky's "O dryani" ("About Trash") a portrait of Marx laments:

> Philistine threads have entangled the Revolution.
> Philistine life is more terrible than Wrangel.
> Quickly
> Grab the canaries and strangle—
> So that communism
> Won't be canaried into dissolution![17]

A desire for such acquisitions was noted together with aristocratic pretentions within the same character. Pretention nourished the desire to acquire first petty bourgeois trinkets and then more impressive possessions.

Perhaps the most distinctive trait of the Nepman was his interest in speculation. Speculation was deeply ingrained and was treated as the norm rather than the exception. Everyone speculated with everything imaginable, from food and fuel to petty trinkets. Speculation in the necessities of life such as food and fuel met with ridicule, while speculation in all other articles was treated with a good deal of humor and satirists emphasized the extent of the activity. Buttons, clothing, shoes, all manner of consumer goods, and even husbands were used. Newcomers to Moscow in Averchenko's *Odessity v Petrograde* (*Odessians in Petrograd*) even attempt to deal in diabetes.

The new philistine was treated by both literary camps. All factions admitted that there was a new Soviet philistine, and all placed his historical roots in Gogol. His immediate roots, however, were disputed. While both camps admitted that the philistine arose during the twenties, proregime satirists attributed his genesis to the influence of the prerevolutionary philistine, as evident in the relationship of Bayan and Prisypkin in "The Bedbug," whereas Fellow Travelers and emigrés implied the lack of change produced by the Revolution and contended that the new Soviet man was in reality the old philistine. The philistine was primarily a phenomenon of NEP and was essentially ignored during War Communism because of the preoccupation with the Revolution. Also the economic deprivation of War Communism stunted the development of the philistine, who flourished only during NEP when conditions were more conducive to his mode of life. Unlike most aspects of contemporary life the philistine was not a purely Russian phenomenon. Proregime satirists applied his stereotyped characteristics, particularly the worship of money, to Western Europe and the United States. The portrayal of the foreign philistine featured much more overt ideology than the indigenous type, primarily because the major vehicle was agitprop.

The major works of the most accomplished satirists for the most part were concentrated on these themes of contemporary life, and, indeed, the daily problems faced by the average person everywhere have traditionally provided a strong impetus for the satirist's pen. A good deal of laughter and irony rather than bitter humor or exposé were evident, and this lighter and freer approach, unencumbered by the militant ideological note associated with the depiction of the Revolution and the Civil War, was perhaps the major contributing factor to the flourishing satire in mid-decade.

5. Foreign Lands and Peoples

SATIRISTS BEGAN to create the image of foreign lands and peoples during War Communism as a result of the political requirements of the Revolution and the intrigues of the Civil War. The United States and Western Europe were the object of the great majority of satirical references because of their political conflicts with the Soviet Union. Traditional national stereotypes were employed where they existed, but a particular Soviet coloration was added based upon revolutionary ideology. This bias tended to produce negative caricatures, to exaggerate traditional faults, and to show life abroad as a combination of exploitation and oppression. Most works dealing with foreign countries were produced by proregime satirists, eager to expose and discredit the West. The remainder was produced either by writers such as Ehrenburg, who had an overriding distaste for certain elements of Western life apart from political considerations, or by Fellow Travelers, who utilized the satirical archetypes for humor.

ENGLAND AND THE ENGLISH

The initial stereotype of the Englishman, the pompous hypocrite, overly concerned with propriety and outward form, was based on clichés existing at the beginning of the Soviet period. The primary source of this figure was Zamyatin, who viewed the English tendencies toward propriety, form, and rules as symptoms of entropy. Exemplary are the two works written in conjunction with his trip to England, *The Islanders* and *Lovets chelovekov* (*A Fisher of Men*).

The principal English stereotypes in *The Islanders* are Vicar Dooley, Kemble, and Lady Kemble. Dooley's insistence upon propriety and form stems from his mathematical approach to life, while Kemble and his mother are products of English tradition. Kemble's narrow, aristocratic approach to life and preoccupation with form are illustrated by his reasoning that "the greatest people in the world are the British; the most heinous crime in the world is to drink tea with the spoon in the cup."[1] Lady Kemble attempts to preserve an atmosphere of elegance, propriety, and order even though the family is impoverished. It was this traditional English image of the Kembles that developed into the Soviet satirical stereotype. Vicar Dooley was too obviously a product of Zamyatin's philosophy to be systematically employed. The Kembles are unique Soviet national stereotypes because they were brought to Soviet satire by a Fellow Traveler. The great majority developed through agitprop.

A *Fisher of Men* proceeds beyond *The Islanders* by demonstrating that the English preoccupation with propriety is but a shield for a tradition-ingrained hypocrisy. The central character is Kraggs, a regular church-goer, a successful banker and investor, and one of the volunteer apostles in the "Society for the Struggle with Vice." Beneath the proper and seemingly irreproachable facade, however, lies a contrasting reality, suggested in part by the unpleasant phonetic impression produced by the name Kraggs. Kraggs significantly enhances his income by patrolling the city parks at night, often on his hands and knees or even on his stomach, to catch people in compromising situations. He allows himself to be bribed for not informing the police or the families involved.

The theme of religion pervades both stories. Part of the facade of propriety is physical presence in church accompanied by a professed insistence upon Christian virtues in life. Lady Kemble and Kraggs are the prime examples of this trait. Ministering to a congregation of Kembles and Kraggses required the appearance of strict propriety and definite rules. Vicar Dooley, the stereotype of the English clergyman, is based upon these requirements. The accepted image of the clergyman in the decade has been described by Valentin Kiparsky: "To them [Soviet Russian writers] they [Anglican clergymen] have appeared as hypocritical, selfish individuals, sadly lacking a personal conscience about what is right and wrong—though they readily preach sanctimonious humbug to wealthy parishioners."[2] The figure of Vicar Dooley was subsequently employed rarely by other satirists, because the focus of foreign stereotypes was political and because the agitprop campaign against religion dealt almost exclusively with Russian Orthodoxy and generalized religious dogma.

The English Lord, the companion of all the Lady Kembles, became the symbol of reaction, political and social evil, bourgeois life style, and the center of anti-Soviet sentiment. He was regarded as the bastion of unenlightened and backward conservatism and made frequent appearances in agitprop literature of the decade. His image was partially derived from the pretentious philistine and partially based on the clichés of English tradition. His presence in longer prose works was limited and relegated to the stereotyped foreigner in league with Soviet villains.

English imperialism was a frequent target of the agitprop satirists. The accusation of imperialism was a political wedge employed against the Western world, but because of the extensive British Empire and its commercial interests throughout the world, the English received the brunt of the attack. Topical references were made about English involvement in China and other countries. The portrayal of Western powers arguing over unclaimed land was a common tactic in exposing imperialism. At the outset of Mayakovsky's "Misteria-Buff" ("Mystery-Bouffe") an Englishman (Lloyd-George) and a Frenchman (Clemenceau) arrive simultaneously at the North Pole, fleeing the allegorical deluge representing October. Each immediately claims the land for his own country, and they begin to fight. Western imperialism became such a common attribute that nonagitprop satirists employed it as an easily recognizable character trait for humor. In Bulgakov's "The Crimson Island" a ship bearing Lord Glenarvan and Monsieur Paganel docks at the island kingdom of Sizi-Buzi. Lord Glenarvan claims the island for England and Paganel for France, and a fight quickly ensues. It is clear that Bulgakov is making use of a cliché with humorous intent, for he had no ideological reason to expose English and French imperialism.

Imperialism, more than any other trait, was used to characterize English political leaders from Disraeli through Lloyd-George to Churchill and Chamberlain. England's participation in the Entente intervention during the Civil War was attributed as much to stereotyped historical imperialistic designs as it was to bourgeois and big-business domination of the government and anti-Soviet sentiment. As indicated in the discussion of the intervention, the political leaders emerged as little more than caricatures and objects of abuse. But even though the abuse was frequently personal, the political leader was regarded more as a symbol than as an individual, more as John Bull than as David Lloyd-George or Winston Churchill.

The English capitalist was intimately involved in imperialism, and although he was not as important as his American counterpart to the

Soviet satirist he was portrayed frequently. It was usually the capitalist who was in league with Russian villains. The portrayal of English capitalism was based in large part on the attempt by English oil interests, particularly Sir Wilhelm Deterding, the transplanted Dutch oil tycoon, to seize control of the massive oil fields of Baku, which before the Revolution were the site of extensive foreign investment. Apart from the agitprop works of Mayakovsky the best example of the English capitalist is in Alexey Tolstoy's *The Emigrés*, originally titled *Chyornoe zoloto (Black Gold)*. The novel depicts English capitalists buying the oil interests of destitute emigré White capitalists and then advocating a war to secure their interests. *The Emigrés* is typical of novels written about foreign capitalism. The characters are much like the caricatures in agitprop verse, and there is no attempt at either a rounded character or a balanced portrayal. The capitalists' attempts to profit from or to undermine the Soviet Union are always unsuccessful, and their Russian colleagues, usually emigrés or White saboteurs, are exposed.

Although capitalists were depicted primarily in the international arena, they were also shown on the domestic front where they regularly abuse the English worker. Proregime satirists, particularly the agitprop faction, attempted to separate foreign workers, considered allies because October was a workers' revolution, from the bourgeois establishment. The plight of these workers was emphasized and embellished, and foreign labor leaders were regarded as exploiters and as extensions of indifferent and greedy capitalists. The image of the labor leaders probably dates back in part to the depiction of Samuel Gompers in Vladimir Korolenko's *Bez yazyka (Without a Voice)* but is primarily a product of War Communism politics. The best example of exposé against the foreign labor situation is Mayakovsky's trilogy of poems—"Anglysky lider" ("The English Leader"), "Moshch Britanii" ("The Might of Britain"), and "Havelock Wilson"—written against Havelock Wilson, the head of the English seaman's union. Wilson is portrayed as being more interested in bourgeois imperialism and big-business establishment interests than in seamen whose lives and working conditions are drawn naturalistically.

Workers' strikes and demonstrations of sympathy for the Soviet regime are the most frequent activities of Mayakovsky's foreign workers, but they gain little by them. It will be remembered that during War Communism, Mayakovsky and agitprop satirists in general portrayed foreign leaders and national stereotypes as ineffective against the new Soviet power. Mayakovsky changed his approach when dealing with the foreign labor movement, and for the most part he concentrates on the abuse endured by the workers and the power of establishment-minded business and labor leaders. Both of Mayakovsky's contentions were realistic, however, even though they were taken for propagandistic reasons. The Entente intervention into the Civil War was a colossal failure, and the socialist movement in Western Europe and the United States met with little success.

The antagonist of the English worker was often the bobby. English police were depicted as extensions of a bourgeois government, vicious apologists for reaction, and enforcers of exploitation. They are commonly shown breaking up workers' demonstrations and strikes and voicing anti-Soviet sentiments. Ehrenburg in *The Stormy Life of Lazik Roytshvanets* adds a further dimension by linking police with imperialism. While in Israel, Laz is beaten and imprisoned as a Bolshevik and then lectured by British police:

> "You exhibit the most shameless lack of gratitude. We have
> given you back your Motherland," they said. "We are protecting
> you. That is called 'the mandate.' Do you understand now? We
> have built a naval port for the British fleet and an air base to serve
> flights from England to India. We stint nothing for you. But we
> will not permit the infection of Bolshevism"(p. 253).

FRANCE AND THE FRENCH

The satirical image of France was produced largely through the vehicle of agitprop and the works of two erstwhile emigrés, Ehrenburg and Tolstoy, who were abroad for some time before returning to the Soviet Union and the good graces of the party. Both devoted a significant portion of their work to life in Western Europe and exposed faults from both personal and ideological points of view. As was true for the image of foreign countries and peoples in general, the image of France was produced with little humor and the emphasis was largely on ideological concerns, the dominant themes being French politics and culture.

The satirical picture of French politics emphasized the historical antagonism toward Germany, imperialism, and the intervention into the Russian Civil War. The antagonism toward Germany stemmed principally from an acute nationalism. In Ehrenburg's *Julio Jurenito*, Monsieur Delais, confronted by the German Karl Schmidt, immediately asks the savage Aysha to kill him. Delais, a man ostensibly devoted to culture and civilization, is prompted by strong nationalistic feelings and a hatred toward Germany which antedates the First World War. This nationalism is grounded in a chauvinistic attitude toward French culture. Ehrenburg portrays a perilous and ironic balance between nationalism, humanitarian civilization, and culture in the novel. He has his protagonist Julio organize the French in an excursion to the statue of a merchant that he has dubbed the Champion of Civilization. The bourgeois people honor this symbol in the name of civilization and culture. But when Aysha returns from combat with a necklace made of the teeth of Germans he has killed, he is acclaimed a hero and given an honorary degree. French nationalism is, therefore, a stronger force than civilization, and both are based in bourgeois culture.

French imperialism stems from this same nationalism and a pseudodevotion to culture. In Ehrenburg's *Trest D. E. (Trust D. E.)* the death of Europe is planned. Ens Boot, the mastermind of the destruction, depends upon existing national animosities to destroy the whole of Europe, and he finds the French particularly susceptible to national hatred and prejudice. Greed augments this petty hatred to give French imperialism the traditional capitalistic aura. Unique to French imperialism, however, was the pompous exporting of culture. Frequently, particularly in the works of Ehrenburg, French international expansion is an attempt to impose a superior culture. This labels the entire country as philistine and explains why the emigré White philistine preferred to settle in Paris. The traditional imperialistic competition between England and France within this context becomes a battle between bourgeois commerce and bourgeois culture. For the proregime satirist the portrayal of such events indicts all concerned. France and England are not alternatives to each other but emanations from the same bourgeois source.

For the Soviet satirist the most important phase of French politics was the participation in the intervention. Culture, nationalism, imperialism, and a hatred for the Bolsheviks motivated French participation in the view of the proregime satirist. The French army and political leaders were shown as inept and the failure of the intervention as predictable. French forces inside Russia during the intervention are shown as a composite of the Whites and existing national stereotypes. They are brutal and unfeeling and resort to needless acts of cruelty. French leaders are depicted through the same stereotypes but feature an added element of pretentiousness reminiscent of the philistine.

The intervention was frequently treated topically by agitprop satirists, and short news items were used as the subject matter of satirical verse. Such an occasion was the French attempt to send relief to war-torn Russia spearheaded by Giraud, a wealthy Moscow industrialist who emigrated; Noulens, the head of an international commission for aid to Russia and a former diplomat to the tsar's court; and General Pau, a French monarchist. In Mayakovsky's "Pesnya pro gostey iz frantsuzskoy oblasti" ("Song of the Visitors from France") and Bedny's "Kak oni golodnym pomogayut; kapitalisty svoi i chuzhie" ("How They Help the Hungry; Foreign Capitalists and Our Own"), the effort as well as the source of the effort are lampooned as insufficient and undesirable.

The image of the French police is an extension of the theme of French politics. French police are portrayed the same as the English bobby and all foreign police. They play the role of enforcers of corrupt government policies and abusers of the workers. In Tolstoy's *The Emigrés* they are depicted as indiscriminately beating French workers who are demonstrating on behalf of their English counterparts. The fact that the French police object to a demonstration on behalf of English workers indicates that they are antilabor and not merely anti-Soviet. This strengthens the contention of proregime satirists that Western governments and the proletariat are incompatible. The most complete portrayal of French police occurs in Olesha's "A List of Blessings." The play was written after *Envy* and suggests an attempt to fall more in line with the party's demands on literature. The play portrays the French police eager to discredit the Soviet embassy and to find an excuse to rout a crowd of unemployed workers, but an elaborate plan proves ultimately unsuccessful in an acceptable ideological conclusion.

French culture, symbolized as the pride of Western civilization, was attacked from several stances. It was linked with nationalism and imperialism and portrayed as a destructive force. It was also denounced as bourgeois. The most frequently satirized aspect of French culture was the bohemian, avant-garde character of Parisian arts and letters. Typical of the presentation is "A List of Blessings." Monsieur Margeret, the manager of a music hall, contracts an ideologically confused Russian actress and suggests to her a vulgar, modernistic approach to "Hamlet" replete with stunts:

First you play the flute . . . any minuet . . . so that the
audience will get in a melancholy mood. There. Then you swal-

low the flute. . . . The audience gasps. A change of mood: surprise, concern. Then you turn your back to the audience, and it
turns out that the flute is protruding out of a place that flutes
never protrude. That's even more zesty since you're a woman.
Now. Listen to me, this is marvelous. Then you start to blow into
the flute, so to speak, backwards—but no longer a minuet, but
something livelier like "Tommy, Tommy, Let's Meet on Tues-
day." Understand? The audience is in ecstacy; laughter; a storm
of applause.[3]

The actress is subsequently introduced to a French singing idol, who
speaks with vulgar innuendoes and immediately tries to arrange a
rendezvous in his apartment. The warped approach to art as well as the
caricatures of immoral Frenchmen close to the arts became clichés and
contrasted effectively with the sober purposefulness of Socialist
Realism.

Paris symbolized not only the degeneracy of the arts but also all that
was objectionable in France. The trait most frequently mentioned by
proregime satirists was the debauchery and profligacy of Parisian life.
Paris entertainment was viewed as a continual round of naked women
performing for the amusement of drunken observers. In *Engineer
Garin's Hyperboloid*, Tolstoy contrasts the wealthy, bourgeois part of
Paris, in which debauchery flourishes, with the large, impoverished
workers' section contiguous to it, which is free of such vice.
Mayakovsky also attacked Paris from a politically motivated moral
stance in "Parizhanka" ("A Parisian Woman") in which he depicts a
woman working in a men's washroom distributing soap and other
necessities in order to make a living. The author comments:

> But it's very
> 　　difficult
> 　　　　in Paris
> 　　　　　　for a woman,
> if
> 　　a woman
> 　　　　doesn't sell herself
> 　　　　　　and works instead.[4]

Loose morals are part of the French national stereotype and are exposed for political reasons rather than moral ones in order to illustrate
bourgeois decadence. The Soviet stereotype thus does not differ mark-

edly from the usual satirical view of the French, but the political
coloration is decidedly Soviet.

AMERICA AND AMERICANS

Although France and England were the satirists' most common subjects immediately following the Revolution, the United States quickly
became the most frequent target as the decade progressed. To the
proregime satirist the United States was the epitome of political abuse
and bourgeois life, in short, of everything the Revolution was against.
The objects, techniques, and rhetoric used in satirizing the United
States were much the same as those used against other foreign nations,
but they were more intense. It was quickly evident that the United
States, because of its political and military influence, was the true
enemy of the Soviet Union, and from the early twenties it has been the
principal target of satire.

Most frequently attacked was the corrupt American capitalist and
businessman. The bourgeois businessmen and kings of huge financial
empires were exposed. The financial kings, who were much more
powerful than their Western European counterparts, received the
most attention. At the outset of the twentieth century Korolenko and
Gorky had portrayed the superrich villain, and Gorky's *Gorod zhyol-
togo dyavola* (*City of the Yellow Devil*) and *Odin iz koroley respubliki*
(*One of the Kings of the Republic*) especially had a significant influence
in forming subsequent portraits. The American millionaire never appeared as the Horatio Alger fairy-tale hero in nonsatirical Russian
literature, while in satirical literature he assumed exaggerated powers
and negative qualities which quickly became stereotyped. The first
work in the Soviet era exposing the American capitalist was Ehrenburg's *Julio Jurenito*, which provided the prototype for a long line of
works against American capitalism. Mister Cool, the capitalist,
exemplifies hypocrisy and a consuming preoccupation with the dollar.
Both of these qualities became attributes not only of the millionaire but
also of the typical American citizen.

Ehrenburg more than any other satirist portrayed the capitalist, and
following *Julio Jurenito* there appeared *Trust D. E.*, a thoroughgoing
indictment of American capitalism. Mister Tvaift, organizer of the best
canned-meat factory in the world, has written a pamphlet called "Our
Moral Obligation, or Reproduce Intelligently from Now On," in which
he demonstrates conclusively that man evolved from the frog. The

exposing of such pedantic and pretentious intellectualism is a traditional satirical device used to belittle a character's mental capabilities. Tvaift is willing to devote part of his millions toward the destruction of Europe for personal and selfish reasons: "He hated Europe because it would not buy his canned meat and reproduce intelligently."[5] A similar readiness is expressed by Jebbs, the steel king from Pittsburgh, who is willing to help finance Europe's destruction when he learns that the price of a steel razor made in Hamburg is twenty cents, while the American version sells for four dollars. The third member of the financial triumvirate is Williams Hardyle, the son of an oil king, who donates his millions simply to be able to honeymoon in private in the postdestruction European wilderness. The financial magnates in such works are referred to as kings in order to demonstrate the power of money in America and the reverence wealthy men command. The callous detachment with which the financiers plot Europe's destruction is strikingly reminiscent of the stereotype of the Communist and the White. The major addition to the image is the selfishness motivated by the monetary greed that became the principal characteristic of the United States and its people. The image of the capitalist is thus reminiscent of both the machine-man and the philistine.

Ehrenburg portrayed another arena of American capitalism, the film industry, in *Fabrika snov* (*The Dream Factory*). His film magnates, all of them European-born Jews, are in the industry to make money, and they engage in fierce competition for viewers. Ehrenburg related ironically and satirically to Jewry in other works because of personal cynicism, and his combination of the capitalist and the Jew in *The Dream Factory* is his own fetish rather than a stage in the development of the stereotype. The large motion picture studios that claim to control the world ironically become mere pawns of the technical corporations that produce their machinery and control their profits. Thus the novel is also an attack upon industrial giants, such as Western Electric, Radio Corporation of America, American Telephone and Telegraph, and General Electric. Such corporate giants were often alluded to by proregime satirists to expose the power wielded by the rich. Ehrenburg portrays the pretentiousness of these corporations by showing their desire for worldwide influence. The pretentions are mocked through a parody of the division of the world between Spain and Portugal by Pope Alexander VI in 1494. Bill Hayes, who has been appointed the tsar of filmdom and who is frequently referred to in religious terms à la Zamyatin's Benefactor, makes the division:

After lengthy discussion the world was finally divided. The Germans were given Central Europe from Scandinavia to the Balkans and also the lowland colonies. 180,000,000 people. This is the empire of "Klangfilm-Tobis-Kuchenmeister." The Americans get the United States, Canada, India, Australia, and Russia. In England there is a dual protectorate: the Americans get three fourths of the profits and the Germans one fourth.[6]

Kataev and Tolstoy subsequently depicted the American capitalist, using Ehrenburg's stereotypes in the main. Kataev's *Erendorf Island* depicts Matapal, a veritable king of kings, who controls much of the commercial and military activity of the Western world. His power stems from his enormous wealth, which he plans to use to rule the world. Adventure novels centering around an American capitalist who uses his millions to finance a devious invention that would put him in control of the world flourished during the middle twenties. Hyperbole was exercised not only in the wealth and power of the capitalist but also in the scientific scheme used to promote his intentions. Tolstoy's *Engineer Garin's Hyperboloid* is another example of this type of work. American business interests conspire with Garin, a Russian villain, to attempt to control the world. The financier of the plot is Rolling, a direct descendant of Mr. Cool. Of interest in the work is the image of the wealthy American businessman, who is on a much lower financial rung than the superrich figures of Matapal and Rolling. In one scene these businessmen congregate in Paris' Hotel Majestic for a conference on trade:

They busily guzzled all kinds of drinks from one morning to the next. Out of thin air their hairy fingers weaved money, money, money. . . . For the most part they crawled in from America, from that cursed country where they are up to their knees in gold, where they are preparing to buy up all of the good Old World as cheaply as possible.[7]

This portrayal of America as a country made filthy by a materialistic perspective began during War Communism. Satirists used this image as their point of departure even when dealing with the superrich.

The agitprop poetry of Mayakovsky and Bedny was important in popularizing the symbols of capitalism and individual American capitalists. Wall Street quickly became a symbol of American exploitation as did financiers like J. P. Morgan and John D. Rockefeller. In the eyes of the agitprop satirist the dollar ruled in America, and the power of the superrich epitomized this. Contrary to typical agitprop technique, men like Morgan and Rockefeller were not treated with the same ferocity which was used in exposing the stereotyped capitalist. Personal references were overshadowed by the fabulous wealth controlled by such men. This differs markedly from the treatment of political figures, who were treated much more crudely than their stereotyped counterparts.

The treatment of America and American life was characterized by a large number of topical references. Calvin Coolidge, Henry Ford, New York City, Broadway, Chicago, the League of Nations, Hollywood, the crime rate, and other institutions, public figures, and incidents were common. The use of topical references, many of them gleaned from American newspapers, were primarily the tool of agitprop writers. Mayakovsky and Bedny eagerly utilized the much publicized Sacco-Vanzetti case and the Scopes trial to indicate the reactionary nature of American life. Topical comments were not confined to agitprop, however. A typical reference is found in *The Dream Factory*, in which Ehrenburg exposes the American penal system:

> In 1875 an inspection revealed that Sing Sing Penitentiary was in violation of the hygiene code and should be destroyed. Fifty-five years have passed. Sing Sing still exists today. The administration wasted three hundred dollars on the installation of an electric chair: this was dictated by humanitarian considerations (p. 178).

The theme of labor, including the use of brutality, was widely used to attack capitalism and received even more attention with reference to the United States than it had in the portrayals of England and France. The satirical villains were the capitalists and the labor leaders who, like Havelock Wilson, were shown to be more concerned with management and the implicit exploitation than with the workers. Samuel Gompers became the symbol of the corrupt labor leader. In the poem "Gompers," Mayakovsky portrays him addressing a crowd of workers:

> It's my advice:
>   that you get rid of all these revolutions!
> One should
>   never
>   quarrel with the Pope.

And we are
   all—
       Rockefeller's children.[8]

This anti-Bolshevik attitude became commonplace for labor leaders in all countries. Henry Ford also became a symbol of the exploiting capitalist and Detroit the symbol of worker abuse. Mayakovsky's naiveté and propagandistic bent are evident in his depiction of Detroit found in *Moyo otkrytie Ameriki (My Discovery of America)*, the result of a trip to the United States in the middle twenties: "Detroit has the highest divorce rate. Ford's system makes the workers impotent."[9]

American treatment of the worker was portrayed with an added dimension not evident in other countries. Soviet satirists exposed racism, real and imagined, to indict the American social structure and the minority worker's status, which was decidedly worse than that of his white counterpart. Mayakovsky's "Blek end uayt" ("Black and White") singled out the sugar and cigar kings for their exploitation of black labor in Havana, while his "Sifilis" ("Syphilis") exposed the difference in treatment accorded the "pork king" Swift and Negro laborers. Racism was not a prominent target for Soviet satire in the twenties, and in general satirists used it only in application to the labor movement in America. Ehrenburg attacked racism in its social rather than political context in *The Dream Factory*, but his work is decidedly an exception.

The official American attitude toward the new Soviet government and the Revolution was shown as the product of reactionary capitalism. The antagonism was portrayed as consistent with American militarism, imperialism, and the archconservative character of American life. The kernel of anti-Soviet sentiment was often found in the American press. Proregime satirists mocked the American press for seeing a Soviet plot in every distressing event and a Soviet spy lurking behind every tree. The similarity between this satirical depiction and the Joseph McCarthy era in the United States Senate several years later is striking. Kataev's *Lunnaya sonata (Moonlight Sonata)* is typical. Professor Vor claims to be inventing a rocket that will land on the moon. American financiers eagerly back the project, but when Vor, as his name would suggest (thief), absconds with the money, the State Department quickly denounces him as a member of the Comintern and the entire plan as a Communist plot to take over the United States.

Tolstoy expanded the image of the press and exposed it as a reactionary prevaricator, an apologist for American sins, and a creator of official myth. In *Engineer Garin's Hyperboloid* the press joins the American government in hailing Garin, who wants to control the world through his death ray, as a liberating dictator and hero. Daily feuilletons create a myth by whitewashing his past and motives and by making him into the "all-American success story." Tolstoy also showed journalistic pre-varication descending to the level of intentional sensationalism. In *Soyuz pyati* (*A League of Five*) he portrays American reporters intrud-ing upon mysterious events on an isolated island. The reporters are irksome, meddling, and devoid of editorial objectivity. Their search for sensationalism reaches absurd proportions as one attempts to outdo the other in producing horror tales about the activities on the island. The foreign press in general was lampooned by Soviet satirists, but none was treated so harshly or so frequently as was the American press.

Irrespective of denomination, the established churches were at-tacked as bastions of reaction, hypocrisy, and all that was typically American and therefore bad. The work that gave impetus to the treatment of the American church was *Julio Jurenito*, with the figure of Mr. Cool. Cool uses the Bible to make a great deal of money and at the same time perpetuates a faith based on expediency. Cool is reminis-cent of Vicar Dooley but has a capitalistic base not considered by Zamyatin. It was Ehrenburg's stereotype that transcended Zamyatin's rather traditional image that became the point of departure for Soviet satirists. Vicar Dooley's ideological foundation was too anti-utopian and too obviously indicated Zamyatin's independent and democratic stance. The image of Cool is extended in *Trust D. E.*, in which millionaire Mormons are shown catering to and seeking the favors of the superrich capitalists intent on destroying Europe. The union of the Bible and the dollar became the foundation upon which the American church functioned in satirical writing, while spiritualism and ritual, frequently lampooned in American satire, never became significant targets. The reason for this is that America was perceived by Soviet satirists almost exclusively from the point of view of capitalism.

OTHER FOREIGN NATIONS

Satirical treatment of foreign nations other than England, France, and America was limited to Germany, as Soviet satirists concentrated on those countries toward which there was political animosity. The satiri-cal treatment of Germany was linked with World War I and was little more than propaganda. Those clichés that had long been applied to Germany were used after the war and little new was added. The prototype of the German was Karl Schmidt in *Julio Jurenito*. Schmidt exhibits a utilitarian and rigidly organized approach to life. He is also characterized by an acute nationalism, more extreme than even the French. These traits are used by Ehrenburg to explain Germany's participation in World War I and the imperialism that gripped that country in the first half of the twentieth century. Schmidt is almost transformed into a German Grand Inquisitor through his insistence that all nations be subject to German rationalism, utilitarianism, and organization for their own well-being and future development. Colonial imperialism was not mentioned as frequently with reference to Germany as it was to France and England, and in general Germany was not made the object of as much satirical writing as the big three of the Entente, thus indicating the close ties between literature and immediate political concerns.

Other foreign nations were never part of a concerted satirical program as were the four major powers of the West, and treatment of them was limited to a large extent to topical references in agitprop works. Typical of such work is Mayakovsky's "Kak rabotaet respublika demokraticheskaya" ("How a Democratic Republic Works"), in which he depicts bourgeois elements fleeing the Revolution into Riga, Latvia. Latvian repression and censorship are subsequently exposed as embarrassing characteristics of a supposedly free democracy. This type of short satirical work was the only type used in the treatment of countries and peoples of minor political interest.

The images of foreign lands and peoples were important in the development of satire during the decade but were largely subordinated to the two main thematic trends, the Revolution and contemporary life. The fact that politics determined the targets makes the exposing of foreign lands and peoples consistent with the tenor of satire during the decade and provides the basis for the connection with the Revolution and contemporary life. Foreign countries are related to October through the Entente intervention and the adherence to the middle-class values opposed by the Revolution. They are related to contemporary life through Soviet villains—the philistine, embezzler, bureaucrat, saboteur—who display bourgeois life styles and who are usually linked with foreign business or political interests.

The portrayal of foreign lands and peoples was dominated by the exposé characteristic of the Revolution and the Communist, and in many ways it grew out of the period of War Communism. The reasons for this portrayal include viewing them in the political context of War Communism, since only those nations with which a political animosity existed were treated. Also most satirists generalized foreign vices, and there was no conflict between the portrayal of universal abuse and isolated individual departures. In this area the agitprop faction dominated production, using stereotypes that were particularly an anathema to revolutionary ideology and were based primarily ·on the White and, to a lesser extent, on the philistine. Thus existing national characteristics and stereotypes were given a political denotation.

Perhaps the pivotal factor was the role played by agitprop, especially by Mayakovsky. The emigrés did not treat these themes because of their overriding preoccupation with the Revolution, resulting living conditions, and the Communist. The Fellow Travelers remained on the level of existing national stereotypes and emphasized humor. The moderate proregime faction produced little. It remained for the agitprop faction to portray those qualities condemned by the Revolution: imperialism, capitalism, and an anti-Soviet attitude. These traits were emphasized as foreign in order to enhance the claim that the Revolution had to a great extent purged Russia of similar sins. To a significant degree the stereotypes were formulated during War Communism, when a bitter tone dominated and when notorious individuals were frequently used in place of the stereotypes. The personal attacks on individual labor leaders and political figures were usually more intense than the mocking of the stereotype.

A further reason for the negative exposé was the role played by Tolstoy and Ehrenburg, who were establishing themselves in the proregime camp in an ideological position between the moderate Kataev and the radical Bedny. Tolstoy's contributions were vindictive and perhaps due to his experiences abroad, though more likely attributable to his willingness to follow the party line. He employed the same political stereotypes but remained above the overt propaganda level. Ehrenburg's *Julio Jurenito* was prompted more by personal biases than by Soviet politics, and his writing during the decade retained an aura of intellectual freedom. His ironic humor remained a unique phenomenon, however.

Julio Jurenito had more influence than any other work upon the formation of the national stereotypes used by Soviet satirists. Ehrenburg fashioned all major national stereotypes except the English, which was provided by Zamyatin through the Kembles. The figures of

Mr. Cool, Monsieur Delais, and Karl Schmidt provided the bases for subsequent characters in prose. Cool was the most important character inasmuch as he served as the inspiration for the American capitalist and religious figure. The only substantial modification of Ehrenburg's stereotypes was the addition of a more overtly pro-Soviet interpretation of the character and his activities.

6. Religious and Other Malefactors

IN THE twenties there were numerous satirical propaganda campaigns carried out against social ills, people, and institutions that were regarded as symbols of the tsarist past. Religion, hooliganism, drunkenness, illiteracy, anti-Semitism, and the kulak were the most important targets. They were initially exposed at the government's behest by agitprop satirists, who used placards, pamphlets, editorials, posters, and leaflets in a mass media campaign. Mayakovsky was the most important contributor, and his verse feuilletons were the strongest literary force in the agitprop campaigns. The issues were not shown solely in a propagandistic light, however, and they were also exposed by moderate proregime and Fellow Traveler satirists. Apart from Mayakovsky the most significant contributor was Zoshchenko, whose treatment of these issues may be viewed as part of his examination of contemporary life.

The issue that most stimulated satirical comment was religion. Antireligious writing developed during the first two decades of the century as a reaction to the mysticism of the Symbolists, as a part of the Futurist approach, and as socialist propaganda. This antireligous literature did not become part of a campaign, however, until the impact of the Revolution was felt: "In the platform of the Russian Communist Party (Bolshevik) approved at the Eighth Party Congress (March 1919) it is noted that 'the Party strives toward the complete destruction of the link between the exploiting classes and the organization of religious propaganda, thereby facilitating the actual liberation of the toiling masses from religious superstitions and organizing the most broad-based scientifically enlightening and anti-religious propaganda.' "[1] The agitprop antireligion campaign intensified in 1920 and remained a high priority for radical proregime satirists throughout the decade. Bedny, Alexander Serafimovich, Nikolay Aseev, Alexander Bezymensky, and numerous hack writers, in addition to Mayakovsky, contributed to the campaign. Even though other literary factions exposed certain aspects of religion, the subject was dominated by Mayakovsky, Bedny, and agitprop works and techniques.

Agitprop satirists directed most of their blows onto the petty Orthodox officiant, the deacon and the village priest. They were used as symbols of the corruption of the priesthood and lack of content of Russian Orthodoxy. Bedny was the greatest single force in the establishment of the Soviet stereotype of the priest, whose image stemmed from satirical portraits in nineteenth-century literature. These portraits were found primarily in the work of the radical civic writers who attacked tsardom and Orthodoxy as co-evils. The figure of the profligate, worldly officiant was already a cliché when socialist writers began a systematic campaign. The primary development in the Soviet period was the application of ideological faults to the existing stereotype, the addition of political sins to human foibles.

Bedny's work in this vein stems from early in the second decade of the century, when he was writing to advance the Social Democratic cause. Several of his poems feature the figure of Father Ipat, a coarse, drunken rogue who has no religious values or characteristics. Bedny endowed his stereotype with hyperbolic vices and created a symbol of profligate life. Perhaps the best example of the treatment of the priest is found in Bedny's "Pro tryokh popov" ("About Three Priests"), which contains the physical characteristics and behavior that became stereotyped during the decade. Exploitation of parishioners, drinking, cursing, sympathy and collusion with the Whites, debauchery, and an unpleasant physical appearance became required characteristics of the priest with the intensification of the antireligion campaign in 1920. It is noteworthy that the majority of the negative traits are personal rather than overtly political and have little or nothing to do with religion. The assertion of collusion with the Whites was the only political comment.

The clergy was included in the vast exploitative class, and efforts were made to demonstrate the various ways in which priests preyed upon the people. The emphasis was placed upon the materialism of the clergy, on attempts to extract money from the people, and on the vast wealth of the church. In "Ot pominok i panikhid/U odnikh popov dovolny vid" ("Only Priests Look Pleased by Requiems and Funeral Feasts"), Mayakovsky ridicules the way priests make money from various ceremonies and rituals, particularly those concerned with death. Other works exposed purchased prayers and profit-making confessionals. Mayakovsky showed the priest as an exploiter largely through direct authorial comment and the use of the vices of Bedny's stereotype. He concentrated on the exploitation inherent in the priestly craft, which was portrayed as bereft of traditional Christian virtues and quite consistent with Mr. Cool's union of the Bible and the dollar. By using the stereotype and including him in the exploiting class, Mayakovsky was able to attack Orthodoxy as an institution rather than attacking individual priests. The church was guilty by association with its capitalistic clergy.

The materialistic and superficially pious officiant, while the principal target of agitprop, was not used by agitprop alone. Satirists of other factions used the same stereotype but varied the ideological perspective according to their particular political stance and literary method. Corruption or folly were emphasized depending upon the intent of the nonagitprop satirist, who usually used the stereotype to produce comedy. Typical of the moderate proregime approach is Ilf and Petrov's *The Twelve Chairs.* Vostrikov, who throughout his ecclesiastical career never lost his desire for material possessions, hears Vorobyaninov's mother-in-law's confession about the diamonds hidden in a chair and immediately joins the search for them, in fierce competition with Vorobyaninov himself and Ostap Bender. Vostrikov is totally obsessed by the fruitless quest and finally goes insane. Ilf and Petrov remain on the level of human foible in the figure of Vostrikov and do not include obvious ideological references. Their intent seems to have been to create humor. However, an ideological interpretation and a generalization of vices lead one back to Mayakovsky's conclusions about Orthodoxy.

Zoshchenko's *The Monastery* is characteristic of the less ideological Fellow Traveler approach. In addition to commenting upon materialism and superficiality of belief, the author reiterates the time-honored stereotyped image of the monastery as a corrupt and immoral institution. The narrator of the work comments:

> Of course it's all true what they say about monasteries—monks are people just like the rest of us: they have wives, won't refuse a drink, and have a good time. But that isn't the issue. That's old hat.
> Here's one thing that happened in a monastery. After this I can't stand to see believers. Their faith is nonsense.[2]

The monastery in question is a very wealthy one that caters to affluent patrons, who donate large sums and are in the process of pretentious repentance for years. Zoshchenko also mocks the ascetic practices of the monks who wear leg irons and eat flies. The avaricious Father Superior's illegal plot to obtain more property for the monastery is fouled by an even more avaricious benefactor who then begins to look elsewhere for repentance. Zoshchenko's mockery of asceticism and the monastery reflects a more ambitious scope than that intended by agitprop satirists, who in the main ignored institutions and zealous religious feeling in favor of the figure of the priest. Fellow Travelers and moderate proregime satirists (emigrés wrote little on the issue) extended the field of satirical vision to encompass most aspects of religion. The fact that religion was mocked so widely by those not immediately involved in the party campaign indicates that by the middle of the twenties religion was a volatile issue demanding a certain level of conformity with the government program and that many members of the intelligentsia had lost faith and confidence in Orthodoxy as an institution capable of meeting physical or spiritual needs.

An exception to the generalization that the religious officiant was presented as a stereotype was evident in 1923 when the case against former patriarch Tikhon was being prepared. Tikhon, who was accused of collaboration with the Whites, was treated with the same maliciousness evident in the portrayal of the political leaders of the Revolution and Civil War. Mayakovsky most enthusiastically took up the cudgel against Tikhon. In "Kogda my pobezhdali golodnoe likho, chto delal patriarkh Tikhon!" ("When We Were Conquering Hunger, What Was Patriarch Tikhon Doing!"), he indicts Tikhon for refusing to contribute the church's wealth to help alleviate the famine during the years of War Communism. In "O patriarkhe Tikhone. Pochemu sud nad milostyu ikhney!" ("About Patriarch Tikhon. Why His Eminence Is Being Tried!"), he attacks Tikhon's complicity with the Whites and his open subversion of the Bolshevik regime.

An important ideological aspect of the antireligious campaign was waged in literature almost exclusively by Mayakovsky, who pointed out the difference between the old religion (Russian Orthodoxy) and the new religion of science. Other agitprop satirists concentrated primarily on discrediting the officiant, and Mayakovsky was essentially alone in propagating science as the new faith. His Futurist experience and personal interest in modern technology were the likely roots of his campaign. In 1923 he published two collections, *Obryady* (*Rituals*) and *Ni znakhar, ni bog, ni slugi boga nam ne podmoga* (*Neither the Quack, nor God, nor the Servants of God Gave Us Aid*), in which he jux-

taposed science and religion for his principal literary device. The critic
Ruzhina comments: "Without exception all of the poems Mayakovsky
included in the two collections assert the inevitability of the triumph of
the scientific *Weltanschauung* as juxtaposed to religious ideology. Science rather than God, says the poet, will help the working man" (p.
161). Mayakovsky flaunted the achievements of science and felt that as
more was learned in the fields of science and technology, the religious
myths and mysteries would fall. He insisted that the socialist man of
the future, the builder, be praised rather than a deity and asserted that
the new Soviet man was the true savior of mankind.

A typical militant poem from these collections is "Ni znakhar, ni bog,
ni angely boga—krestyanstvu ne podmoga" ("Neither the Quack, nor
God, nor the Angels of God Helped the Peasantry"), which is con-
structed through juxtapositions of the reactions of science and religion
with the problems of life: when a drought grips the country, one village
prays while another uses science to compensate for it; when cows get
ill, Fyokla prays while Akulina resorts to books and a veterinarian;
when sickness strikes a village, medicine succeeds where home cures,
superstition, and religion fail. The poem concludes with a rather irreverent comparison of Christ and communism:

> Or does Christ watch over
>   only commercial interests?
> For so many years
>   the peasant
>   has piously crossed himself,
> but got land
>   not from God,
>   but from the communists!
> If Christ has
>   not only long hair,
> but also
>   a mind
>   omnipotent,—
> why
>   is hunger permitted on the Volga?[3]

Mayakovsky was the only agitprop satirist who, even on this superficial level, approached theology as well as religion. His motivation,
however, was based more on politics than on an interest in the ultimate
questions of life. He indicates that the Orthodox God has not attended

to the needs of the peasant and worker and has permitted natural disasters to afflict the people. Mayakovsky here assumes, at least for artistic purposes, that there is a God, something his fellow agitprop satirists either discredited or ignored, but he creates an atmosphere of dissatisfaction and suggests communism as an alternative. His role in the mass media campaign was essentially the same as his cohorts', but the issues he raised were sometimes based on somewhat deeper thinking.

To discredit religion not only because of its inferiority to science but also its incompatibility with the new values of Soviet life, the religious ordinances, doctrine, and rituals were mocked as devoid of meaning, as farcical, exploitative, and harmful. Mayakovsky was most prominent in examining this dimension of religion also. He mocked baptism, marriage, and other ceremonies as little more than silly customs. To accomplish this he contrived situations that made the ceremonies appear absurd: a girl dies after having been baptized with cold, filthy water; another is christened with the uncommon name of an obscure saint and is never able to marry because of it; a bride is forced to marry a much older man she does not love in an elaborate church wedding. These unfortunate instances are juxtaposed to examples of socialist efficiency and humanism. Orthodoxy is thus accused of placing ritual above human life and happiness and of being doctrinaire.

Using the new religion of science and the discredited Orthodox doctrine and ritual as points of departure, Mayakovsky portrays the new Soviet order in "Mystery-Bouffe," one of the first satirical plays in the Soviet era. The work is done in the guise of a medieval morality play, a technique that allows Mayakovsky at once to mock religion and to present a new ethic. It is noteworthy that he attacks religion in general and not specifically Orthodoxy. This departure from the general direction of antireligious satire is necessary here because of the new ethic proposed. Although he usually juxtaposed science to Orthodoxy, such works were written after he published "Mystery-Bouffe," which first demonstrated the need for new directions. The myth of the flood and Noah's ark are used to give a biblical aura to the floodlike spread of the Revolution over the face of the earth. The Revolution-flood cleanses the earth and prepares the way for the new ethic. A Christ figure, claiming to be a man from the future, walks upon the water and offers a new Sermon on the Mount, advocating a physical, earthly paradise. The gods and angels in heaven, the symbols of Orthodox religion, are ineffectual against the Unclean, the bearers of the Revolution, who use for electrification the holy lightning bolts sent down in godly wrath upon the unbelievers. Through the use of the Clean and the Unclean, Mayakovsky ridicules traditional religious purity and virtue, which are unimportant in the building of the new order. The symbolic replacement of the Christian gospel with a new terrestrial ethic of collectivization and electrification indicates the total inadequacy of religious teaching for modern life.

Bedny's *Novy zavet bez izyana yevangelista Demyana* (*The Evangelist Demyan's Flawless New Testament*), in which he undertakes to write the truth about Christianity in view of contradictions in the Four Gospels, was one of the few other works to offer an alternative to religion. The alternative is similar to that of Mayakovsky in "Mystery-Bouffe" but is presented in a much more irreverent and ambitious manner. Bedny indicts the church fathers for deception and claims to have in his possession the Gospel of Judas, which contains the truth. The work is an elaborate rewriting of Christian myth from the birth of John the Baptist through Jesus' ministry to the Resurrection. For the only time in the decade the myths of the birth, Transfiguration, betrayal, Last Supper, atonement, Crucifixion, Resurrection, and miracles are examined in depth. All are summarily dismissed as hoaxes, and plausible explanations are offered. Bedny portrays the historical personage of Jesus as an extention of the image of the profligate village priest found in "About Three Priests." The same clichés are employed but are intensified to make Jesus more reprehensible than the simple priest. Bedny does not confine the presentation to hyperbolic personal foibles and adds a decisive ideological element. He equates Jesus with Rasputin and Christianity with tsardom to emphasize the exploitation and failure inherent in each. The work marks the apex of the agitprop antireligion campaign as it discounts Christian tradition, advances the available stereotypes, combines human foibles with revolutionary ideology, and provides an alternative to religion.

As the decade progressed and the agitprop campaign against alcohol intensified, the themes of religion and alcohol were often linked to form a more effective indictment. Rituals were frequently described as little more than drunken orgies, and works such as Mayakovsky's "Dva opiuma" ("Two Opiums") exposed religion and alcohol as equal scourges upon society. Religious holidays were portrayed as drunken brawls. The linking of alcohol and religion is merely an extension of the nineteenth-century stereotype of the drunken village priest. Satirists who used this theme seldom sought to infuse overt ideology into their works but preferred to let the spectre of the drunken priest and the rowdy holidays speak for themselves. This same tendency is evident in other areas of the campaign and indicates that the purpose of the satirist was often only to discredit. There was frequently no alternative offered and no overt indication of the purpose of the indictment.

Institutionalized Western religion was the object of diatribes from sources spanning the entire spectrum of Soviet satire. Zamyatin, Romashov, Tolstoy, and Ehrenburg exposed the organized church for different reasons yet in much the same fashion. In the view of the satirist, hypocritical clergymen operate organizations that exploit people. The core of exploitation was seen in Ehrenburg's union of the Bible and the dollar. This union was the main point of attack on the church as a social and supposedly humanitarian institution. The Western church was portrayed as an integral part of the bourgeois social structure and a front for anti-Soviet forces. Popular Western targets were the Baptist and Roman Catholic churches and the concept of the Vatican as an independent political entity. Religion was regarded as an ideological and intellectual crime used as a Western characteristic not only because of its inherent evil but also to expose the West by association. Since religion was a negative social phenomenon, a successful indictment was achieved simply by showing the popularity and power of religion in the West, and there were only minor attempts to attack religion on doctrinal grounds. Although religion in the West was castigated, it comprised a small part of the total campaign, which devoted most of its barbs to Russian Orthodoxy. Orthodoxy received the brunt of the attack because it posed an immediate threat to total devotion to Communist principles and the state.

None of the other malefactors to appear in satirical literature received the attention that the priest did. The secondary issues were also dominated by Mayakovsky and agitprop, but Zoshchenko made significant contributions by exposing the social problem connected with the figures of the hooligan, kulak, drunk, illiterate, and anti-Semite, and in mocking the Soviet effort to correct them simplistically.

The campaign against hooliganism was precipitated by the alarming rise in the crime rate during the decade and by the fact that many representatives of the younger generation were taking advantage of the more relaxed atmosphere of NEP. Hooliganism was widespread in both urban and rural areas. While part of the crime wave can be explained by the poverty and physical deprivation afflicting the Soviet Union, hooliganism was more a reflection of the turmoil and violence of the recent past and of the criminal elements in society. The campaign reached its zenith in the middle twenties and continued until the purges of the ensuing decade. Mayakovsky, in such poems as "Khuligan" ("The Hooligan"), "Besprizorshchina" ("Neglect"), "V mirovom masshtabe" ("On a World Scale"), and "Stoyashchim na postu" ("To Those on Guard"), attacked hooligans for the harm they did to the new regime and criticized judges who did not issue strict enough penalties. Hooliganism on the home front was compared to Western imperialism and exploitation on the international scene, and Mayakovsky called for the immediate eradication of both forces. He abandons humor in his attack on the hooligan. With Juvenalian indignation he resorts almost exclusively to authorial comment. He seldom shows the hooligan in action but in a lecturing tone identifies those aspects of the issue that concern him most. His verse on this topic significantly resembles an irate citizen's letter to the editor.

The hooligan's activities were criticized for two principal reasons: they were detrimental to public safety, and they delayed the orderly implementation of communism. The image of the hooligan was somewhat amorphous. He was totally faceless, possessed no readily recognizable physical characteristics, and stemmed from no commonly used stereotype. The agitprop portrayal of the hooligan concentrated almost exclusively on his effect on society, thereby condemning attitudes and actions rather than people. The reason for this anonymity was that the hooligan was difficult to identify and label for any political advantage. As a result his social origin was never made an issue. He was seldom juxtaposed to a positive force such as the Komsomol (Young Communist League), and the totally negative impact conveyed a sense of the urgency of reform.

The kulak was one of the original class enemies singled out by revolutionary rhetoric, but immediately after the Revolution he was frequently lumped with other evil characters and was seldom exposed individually. At the outset of the Soviet era he held a low priority compared to the issues of religion and the Whites, but he gained prominence with the food shortage during War Communism; after the advent of widespread collectivization in 1928, he became one of the most important satirical stereotypes. Mayakovsky's "Litso klassovogo vraga" ("The Face of a Class Enemy") and Bedny's "Mnogo u nas kulakov, a yeshchyo bolshe . . ." ("We Have A Lot of Kulaks and Then Some . . .") are examples of the later work. A short time later the kulak was also treated in some major literary works, such as Kataev's *Vremya vperyod!* (*Forward, O Time!*) and Mikhail Sholokhov's *Podnyataya tselina* (*Virgin Soil Upturned*), which used the stereotype established by the agitprop campaign and resulted from the marshaling of literature into state service during the first Five-Year Plan.

Mayakovsky's treatment of the kulak differs from his approach to the hooligan. He shows the kulak in action: his kulaks exploit poor peasants, attempt to thwart collectivization, and in general play the role of provincial villains. They closely resemble the Whites, and he refers to their activities as evil, both socially and politically. Mayakovsky also adds numerous authorial comments to his verse; these comments are usually political in nature and serve to emphasize the difference between the new ideologically conscious Soviet man and the kulak.

Initially the kulak was exposed because of his wealth and the power he wielded in the villages. His wealth immediately marked him as an exploiter and a bourgeois, while his power posed a real threat to the implementation of communism in the rural areas. He was a remnant of the past who was both annoying and dangerous in the present. Unlike the hooligan the kulak was closely linked with Orthodoxy. This association also implied a connection with tsardom and completed an interesting parallel in which power and religion were regarded as partners. Zamyatin had come to the same conclusion in *We*. The social origin of the kulak was important to the satirist, for it provided a ready example of the effect produced by class enemies. Even though the kulak was a peasant, his association with wealth and religion had transformed him into an exploiter and an enemy of the people. Because of these factors the kulak was portrayed almost exclusively in a political light.

In addition to the priest, the hooligan, and the kulak, the alcoholic was the subject of satirical exposé. The public admission by the Soviet Union that alcoholism remains a serious national problem resurrects the spectre of the satirical campaign waged against drinking in the twenties. The major contributors were Zoshchenko and Mayakovsky. Mayakovsky attacked drunkenness as both an unfortunate human foible and an objectionable anti-Soviet vice by showing its personal and social consequences. He did not contend that drunkenness was an attribute solely of class enemies, and in fact it was a stereotyped characteristic only of the religious officiant. He portrayed it as a widespread practice among peasants and workers and showed it to be partially responsible for hooliganism and the rising crime rate. In this sense he approached it as a general social problem that needed rectifying. This is another instance of Mayakovsky's assuming the stance of the concerned citizen. But he also made drunkenness a political issue. In "Von samogon!" ("Down with Home-Brew!") he claims that class enemies are encouraging the people to drink in order to undermine the regime. Mayakovsky also attempted to shame people by showing the incompatibility of drink and revolutionary principals and the damage it caused to the Soviet Union. He pleaded with, threatened, reasoned with, ridiculed, and disgraced the drinker, but history indicates that his and others' efforts to curb drunkenness were largely failures.

Zoshchenko wrote a number of works on the subject of drinking in conjunction with his portrayal of the panorama of Soviet life. Stories such as *Limonad* (*Lemonade*), *Silnoe sredstvo* (*A Strong Measure*), *Blednolitsye bratya* (*Pale Brothers*), and *Sprysnul* (*Let's Celebrate*) convey the strong influence that alcohol has on the people. Zoshchenko depicted addiction with a good deal of humor, largely ignored by Mayakovsky, but accompanied by a sober undercurrent that effectively transmitted the tragedy of the topic. In *Zemletryasenie* (*The Earthquake*) he exposes not only the subject of drunkenness but also the agitprop campaign waged against it. Snopkov is a cobbler in Yalta at the time of the great earthquake; true to his profession he gets drunk and sleeps through the disaster. He awakes greatly confused, and when he is informed about what happened he vows never to drink again. Adhering to the requirements of propaganda, Zoshchenko delivers his moral together with an aside to the party mass media attack:

> What does the author want to say with this artistic work? With this work the author comes out energetically against drunkenness. The sting of this artistic satire is aimed right at carousing and alcohol.
> Or, as one poster indicates: "Don't drink! Through drunken eyes you might embrace your class enemy!"[4]

Somewhat different from these malefactors were the illiterate citizen and the anti-Semite, who were not so objectionable to the satirist and who were therefore exposed less frequently. The ambitious government project to produce a literate nation as quickly as possible was supported by proregime satirists, who encouraged and mocked those citizens who were still illiterate. Agitprop satirists portrayed class enemies as opposed to the literacy drive because illiteracy was a way to keep the masses in subjugation. Bedny, in such works as "Ne zabyvayte bezgramotnykh bratiev" ("Don't Forget Your Illiterate Brothers"), was the principal contributor to what emerged as the most successful of the agitprop efforts. Significant advances were quickly achieved in eradicating illiteracy, but some Fellow Traveler satirists questioned the striking government claims of success. Zoshchenko's *Tuman* (*Fog*) expressed doubt that deadlines had actually been met and quotas filled:

> But really, citizens, there is no way you can tell now who is literate and who isn't.
> For example, one citizen knows how to sign his name with a flourish, but in general he doesn't know how to write. Another citizen knows how to write, but can't read what he has written. And he's not the only one who can't read it. Give it to a learned professor, and the learned professor won't be able to make head nor tail of it. It doesn't matter that he is a professor. What's written looks like chicken scratches or a dead fly's mess.[5]

Zoshchenko's stories dealing with literacy expose the propaganda aspect of the success claims and depict a project at best only partially complete.

Anti-Semites were made the object of a newspaper campaign during the decade and were exposed as a social evil and a departure from revolutionary principles. Propaganda was contributed by party functionaries, and the bulk of the campaign was editorial. Mayakovsky contributed several verse fueilletons, among them "Zhid" ("Kike"), in which he attacked those who used the word and called for the cooperation of all in ending discrimination. The satire in such verses was decidedly Juvenalian, and very little humor was used during the entire campaign. In longer works, such as *The Adventures of Nevzorov, or Ibikus*, anti-Semitism was portrayed in an ideological light by using it as a characteristic of negative White elements. It was in this vein that anti-Semitism was used in the longer satirical works of the decade, and there was no major satirical effort based exclusively on anti-Semitism. It should be pointed out that this campaign ran counter to a traditional dislike and distrust of Jews on the part of some elements of Russian society and that the campaign itself was by and large a failure. Anti-Semitism smoldered during the thirties and the Second World War, but it flared up again in the anticosmopolitanism and antibourgeois nationalism campaigns that marked the beginning of the Zhdanov era in Soviet literature in 1946.

7. Literature

THE TWENTIES witnessed heated polemics among groups exhibiting a great variety of literary and political postures and appealing to the new Soviet government for official sanction. Party bosses, however, disagreed among themselves about the place of the arts, the direction they should take, and the role of the party in regulating them. This temporary indecision resulted in a good deal of confusion and polemic but also produced a relatively free literary atmosphere. Groups of the literary right (principally the advocates of a proletarian or peasant culture administered and insured by party control) and the left (aesthetic and "formalistic" groups) sought hegemony, while moderate groups of all persuasions advocated an open approach for all. The mixture of politics and aesthetics was confusing, since groups of the literary right were usually on the political left, while the aesthetic fringe of the literary left was normally on the political right (with the exception of the Futurists). The relative freedom endured until the final years of the decade but was continually marred by ideological and aesthetic battles among the various groups.

Despite the fact that there were several politico-literary factions contending among themselves, the basic issues involving literature divided them into two large, quite heterogeneous camps. Factions associated themselves with these camps for both political and aesthetic reasons, but because aesthetic considerations were deemed somewhat more important the composition of the camps was much more complicated than the basic proregime and antiregime opposition characterizing satire during the decade. Generally those who demanded artistic freedom, even though they may have been devoted to the new regime, assumed one position, while those who placed politics above their craft, even though they may have been accomplished artists, assumed the opposite. "Position" was defined politically. What may be termed the aesthetic camp opposed government strictures on literature, al-

116

though its members differed on the acceptable degree of government involvement in the arts. The opposing political camp generally accepted and even invited controls. The aesthetic camp claimed emigré, Fellow Traveler, moderate proregime, and certain "independent" satirists such as Ehrenburg. The political camp contained primarily agitprop and proletarian satirists. These camps were tenuous coalitions at best and were based almost exclusively on the issue of aesthetics.

The literary and political postures of all factions were satirized by rival factions in both camps. The factions which advocated a new peasant or proletarian culture were the most extreme politically and aesthetically and were the frequent targets of the aesthetic camp. The new culturists insisted that only the workers and peasants had the right and the ability to create following the proletarian revolution. They actively solicited artistic contributions from members of these classes and organized formal instruction in writing and painting in the factories and warehouses and on the state farms. Such projects resulted in the mass production of works of questionable value, and thousands of would-be Pushkins and Repins entered the arts. The majority of the new artists were poets—there had been a tremendous outpouring of poetry during and after the war.

The aesthetic camp attacked efforts to stimulate mass production and insisted that such practices were a threat to true creativity. The emigré satirist Don-Aminado in "Nauka stikhoslozhenia" ("The Science of Writing Verse") cites the cliché that "anyone can write poetry," and as an illustration he refers to the thousands of workers and peasants who became poets in the Soviet Union following the Revolution. In *Perepiska s nachinayushchimi (Correspondence with Beginners)* he takes issue with the way these new poets are produced: "if in Soviet Russia one proletarian writer is found in every one thousand illiterates, then in emigré Russia it must be exactly the opposite: for every one thousand writers there is one illiterate."[1]

Several moderate proregime and Fellow Traveler satirists said that workers and peasants attempted to enter the arts simply for economic betterment and to take advantage of modish cultural theories. This tactic was used to mock the proletarian and peasant groups that indiscriminately berated all nonproletarian and nonpeasant writers. Zoshchenko's *Krestyansky samorodok (A Peasant Talent)* portrays a peasant who resorts to writing verse because of severe economic straits and unsuccessfully attempts to use his social origin to insure publication. Zoshchenko uses the economic theme to indicate that the peasants themselves are not convinced of the necessity or efficacy of a peasant culture. However, the moderate proregime faction stressed a different ideological coloration. These satirists depicted undesirable social elements profiting from efforts to produce peasant and proletarian literature. Kataev's *Yemelyan Chernozemny* (*Yemelyan Blacksoil*) and Ilf and Petrov's *The Twelve Chairs* portray bourgeois types and hack writers who attempt to profit by citing deprived social origins and by producing modish work of no value. Kataev, Ilf, and Petrov directed their satirical barbs at abuses rather than at the entire effort to promote proletarian and peasant consciousness. As a result, in the aesthetic camp, conflict persisted between universality and individual abuse. These moderate proregime satirists were hardly proletarians, yet they were not so critical of certain revolutionary tendencies as were Zoshchenko and, particularly, Don-Aminado.

The aesthetic camp feared that the acceptance of the platform of the proletarian groups would result in "pedestrianization" of the arts. The Fellow Traveler and emigré factions linked the party's early efforts to be involved in the arts with the proletarian program. Their thesis was that the Revolution and the subsequent attempts to implement communism cheapened the arts because of political and social tendentiousness, and they cited as evidence the widespread insistence on the proper ideological content, positive values and characters, and a moral. Zamyatin's original accusation that literature would become the handmaiden of the state precipitated the satirical reaction to what ultimately became the doctrine of Socialist Realism. His allegorical treatment of the fate of literature and the arts under absolutism in a negative utopian context was perhaps the earliest objection to controls. Other satirists in the aesthetic camp subsequently explored the issue but did so in the setting of contemporary Russia. Zamyatin's development of the theme at the outset of the decade is evident in "The Fires of St. Dominic" and *We*. In the former, Munebraga, the Inquisitor, is informed of the latest ode written to him and comments: "Yes, this of course is not Petrarch. But . . . to make up for it the author exhibits a slavish devotion to the church, and that makes him superior to Petrarch. . . ."[2]

Absolute devotion to the church, the analogue of the state, becomes the supreme requirement of literature and is made to compensate for artistic mediocrity. Zamyatin demonstrated in *We* the consequences that occur when the state and art are the same in content. R–13, a look-alike of Pushkin and one of the state poets, pens a stanza praised

as "a rare gem for its beauty and depth of thought." The work is a
nonsensical, yet shocking, example of art's future under absolutism:

> Two times two—eternal lovers,
> Eternally fused into passionate four,
> The most flaming lovers in the world—
> Inseparable two times two. . . .[3]

The allusion to the mathematical formula emphasizes the fact that
under absolutism literature must be content with a restricted, rational
approach to reality. The subsequent removal of fantasy through a
compulsory operation makes the novel an important comment on
literary as well as political freedom. The removal of the creative spark
and the required reliance on a rational, objective approach ultimately
resulted in Socialist Realism. Zamyatin prophesied the fate of Soviet
literature, and like most prophets he was condemned in his own
country. Prompted by R–13's verse, D–503 discusses poetry and the
advances it has made since it came under state control: "Now poetry is
no longer the unpardonable call of a nightingale: poetry is service to
the state, poetry is usefullness."[4]

The United States' demand for rationality in literature was translated
into the Soviet demand for ideology. For the most part, the proregime
members of the aesthetic camp emphasized the humor evident in an
overzealous demand for ideological relevancy. But even though
satirists such as Ilf and Petrov shrouded their portrayal in humor and in
general supported the regime, a sharp note of dissatisfaction was
evident. In *The Golden Calf* they depict Sinitsky, an elderly writer of
riddles and puzzles, who is unsuccessful in the Soviet era because he is
unable to infuse his work with sufficient ideology. The very fact that it
was deemed necessary for such writing to contain ideology is the crux
of Ilf and Petrov's complaint, and on certain issues their aesthetic spirit
dominated their political mind.

Ehrenburg's independent stance early in his career typified the
Fellow Travelers' reaction to the imposition of ideology. Already in
1920–21, with the writing and publication of *Julio Jurenito*, he implied
a devotion to artistic freedom and exposed the results of an exclusively
ideological literature. Ehrenburg thus rivaled Zamyatin as the first to
mock the Revolution's impact on the arts and to forecast disaster. In
Julio Jurenito, Tishin, the stereotype of the Russian intellectual, returns to Russia after the Revolution and finds a position teaching
literature to a group studying military economics. The students,

thoroughly indoctrinated with Soviet ideology, want Tishin to lecture about heroes of labor who surpass quotas rather than about Lermontov and Chekhov. This pedestrianization of not only literature but also men's minds was also expressed in *The Stormy Life of Lazik Royt-shvanets*, when Ehrenburg singled out the radical *Na postu!* (*On Guard!*) group. *On Guard!* was the journal published by *Oktyabr* (*October*), the literary group that carried the proletarian banner after the demise of *Proletkult* (*Proletarian Culture*) and before the formation of RAPP (Russian Association of Proletarian Writers). In the novel Lazik meets Arkhip Stoyky, an *On Guard!* writer, who quotes a passage from his latest novel, *The Hum of the Soap-Mill*, as an example of how works are currently being written:

> The hum of the soap was like iron honeybees. With a valiant toss of his head Senka Puvak cried: "That's done it, my lads, the situation's saved." Dunya smiled at his side, and gazed with pride at the driving belts, while the red star rose and fell on her bosom, swollen with healthy enthusiasm. The soap bubbled. "We'll supply the whole Union," declared Senka. He turned his eye to the star on the girl's breast: "Well, Dunya," he cried, "shall we be going? Ours is the path of the young class to the sun. Let us forget the dirty amusement of those who once owned this factory. Let me crush you to my bosom with my arms of labour." And Dunya, abandoning herself to the pulse of new life, a faint blush on her cheeks, whispered: "Look, we have beaten the pre-war norm. Hum on, oh soap, hum on! If it's a boy, we shall call him simply Soap-Hum!"[5]

Ehrenburg's parody reflects the fact that many writers felt threatened by the new literary requirements. Satirists particularly objected, since the applied strictures ran counter to satire by demanding affirmation and by limiting exposé to predetermined targets.

The proletarian poem, replete with positive socialist clichés, ideological or industrial thematics, and derivative Mayakovskian rhythm and rhyme, was also frequently parodied. Ehrenburg ridiculed this movement which was very chic in the poetic generation of the early twenties. His dislike for Mayakovsky and his independent attitude toward art prompted the indictment. In *The Racketeer*, Mishka Lykov, who becomes temporarily infused with Bolshevism under the influence of the adventure and turbulence of War Communism, decides to become a poet. The results are artistic failures typical of the time:

The fact that the result was nonsense didn't bother the young author at all. After all, was the poetry of other poets, even the most celebrated, understandable? No, the issue wasn't sense but rather complex rhyming combinations.

There were so many works written in the first years of the Revolution by bearded schoolboy proletkultists, dreamy trade-schoolers or Red Army men pining over their sweethearts, in which an iamb knocked heads with an anapest and *"pravda"* was rhymed with *"goda."*[6]

Official insistence upon a Marxist interpretation of literature regardless of author, subject matter, or historical context was also mocked by the aesthetic camp, with emphasis on the absurd. In *The Stormy Life of Lazik Roytshvanets*, Ehrenburg's hero is given the hopeless task of writing a Marxist preface to a book translated from the French and dealing with homosexuality and other forms of perversion. Perhaps the most humorous example of Marxist interpretation is found in Don-Aminado's *U lukomorya dub zelyony* (*By the Shore of the Bay Stands a Green Oak Tree*). The work depicts a lecture on Pushkin delivered to the Young Communist League. The lecturer's purpose in speaking to the youth is the rhetorical "What have we done to perpetuate his [Pushkin's] memory from the point of view of the dictatorship of the proletariat?"[7] The initial four lines of "Ruslan i Lyudmila" ("Ruslan and Lyudmila") are used as the basis of the presentation: "By the shore of the bay stands a green oak tree;/A golden chain is on the oak;/And day and night a learned cat/Walks ceaselessly around on the chain."[8] The lecturer asserts that Pushkin's work has deeper meaning because of the severe censorship operative at that time. He cites tsarist imperialism, the attempt to inhibit the masses' self-consciousness, and the exploitation of labor in a flurry of humorous clichés, and he triumphantly reads the lines as Pushkin intended:

> Near the Baltic Sea Naval Base stands a red ash,
> A steel chain is on the ash.
> The eight-hour day for work is great,
> And, by the way, that cat is out of place.[9]

Soviet journalism and the official press were also cited as examples of the damage wrought by controls. While the Western press was satirized for sensationalism and an anti-Soviet attitude, the Soviet press was indicted for excessive ideology, contrived positivism, and dull style. The press was exposed by all factions of the aesthetic camp. Only the agitprop faction, which was subject to dictated priorities and which supported the political bent of journalism, did not participate. Indeed, many agitprop satirists were part or full-time journalists, and the press was the most important disseminator of agitprop campaigns. Ilf and Petrov complain in *The Twelve Chairs* that all journalists write in the same hackneyed, dust-covered phrases about construction and stretch the truth to glorify achievements. As if to test Ilf and Petrov's assertion, Professor Preobrazhensky in Bulgakov's *Heart of a Dog* conducts an experiment to see what effect reading *Pravda* has on his patients. The subjects lose weight, become nervous, and suffer a loss of reflexes because of the ordeal. Both works intimate that the problem is widespread, and there is no conflict in the two between universality and individual abuse. One of the most complete pictures of the press appeared in Bulgakov's *The Fatal Eggs*. After his announced discovery of the mysterious red ray, Professor Persikov is besieged by reporters despite his efforts to avoid them. This recalls the portrayal of the American newspapermen as rude intruders in Tolstoy's *A League of Five*. Over his objections Persikov is interviewed by a GPU journalist, but he treats him rudely and tells him nothing. The reporter unabashedly writes an elaborate article stating that Persikov is very condescending and is eager to share his discoveries with the proletariat.

The aesthetic camp often used direct condemnation to object to such ideological gymnastics, the mechanical inclusion of chic themes and characters, and the resulting poor literary quality. But more common was the rhetorical apology, issued most notably and frequently by Zoshchenko. With this device the satirist expressed mock contrition for not devoting his work to the fashionable themes of the day, usually agitprop targets such as literacy and alcohol, and excused the poverty of his own subject, which in no way contributed to the solution of pressing national problems. The implication is that the reader needs a rest from the common themes of the day. In *M. P. Sinyagin*, Zoshchenko rhetorically apologizes for writing about private life and personal themes when the scarcity of packing materials and the building of silos may be more important. Ehrenburg in *The Racketeer* also attempts to justify his concentration on the negative Mishka Lykov instead of the ideologically acceptable brother Artyom by citing the fact that he is a writer and a satirist, thereby implying the necessity of a certain degree of artistic independence. This technique attacked both the party requirement for relevance and proper ideology and the willingness of the majority of writers to produce works within these guidelines.

The fact that Zoshchenko, Ehrenburg, and others commented upon their departure from chic themes and issues reflects the force with which the new considerations had invaded the literary world and the prevailing attitude among writers concerned with aesthetics and independence that these considerations had already had a debilitating influence on literature. It was only after Stalin's death, again through the work of Ehrenburg in *Ottepel* (*The Thaw*), that the questions of independent choice of theme and technique were raised again with any degree of success.

An additional target of the aesthetic camp was censorship. Even though official circles were somewhat undecided about the role of the party in literature, the censor leaned toward the proletarian factions by insisting upon the inclusion of proper revolutionary ideology, a relevant, contemporary milieu, and positive resolutions. The fact that censorship was an appendage of the supposedly uncommitted party indicated unexpressed official feelings. Satirists frequently attacked such requirements and insisted that they cheapened and weakened literature, but they seldom referred to censorship either directly or allegorically in their writings.

An exception was Bulgakov's play "The Crimson Island," which was quickly driven from the stage and was never published, a victim of the censorship it had mocked. The arbitrary power of the censor coupled with his extreme sensitivity to ideological considerations were the principal factors exposed by the play. "The Crimson Island" deals with the problems of staging a play while under ideological constraints. In the concluding scene, as the censor arrives to observe the rehearsal, the orchestra quickly changes the music from "Oh, It's a Long, Long Way to Tipperary," which the scene calls for, to "We All Come from the Common People." Despite such efforts, the play, an inoffensive allegory of October, is banned as counterrevolutionary. The final scene is changed to show English sailors in mutiny, thereby giving the impression of international solidarity and revolution. The censor passes the revised version but for no expressed reason bans it for all cities except Moscow. Bulgakov insinuates that the necessity of catering to an arbitrary power has a debilitating effect on literature, and a downbeat conclusion emerges despite the extensive humor.

In addition to exposing the threat posed by governmental controls, the aesthetic camp mocked literary trends and figures of both the nineteenth and twentieth centuries. The factions of the camp showed some diversity in choosing targets and applying politics, but generally they mocked these targets from a literary perspective. Usually the satirist intended to produce a humorous allusion or to relate a personal aesthetic opinion. Kataev's *Zolotoe pero* (*The Golden Pen*) and *Bezdelnik Eduard* (*Edward the Loafer*) expose the Turgenevian aristocrat and the transcendental romantic poet, respectively. The two protagonists are hopelessly out of tune with contemporary Soviet reality, and Kataev exposes them from both a political and a literary point of view. He expresses personal dislike for the literary approaches and indicates that they are not valid because of the political change. In *M. P. Sinyagin*, Zoshchenko comments on the lyric poets of the late nineteenth and early twentieth centuries. The protagonist is an outdated remnant of the nineteenth century and resembles in his own way the stereotyped superfluous man. His poetry poorly imitates that of Alexander Blok, Semyon Nadson, and Afanasy Fet, who had become decidedly passé in the twenties.[10]

While the satirical treatment of poetic technique dominated, there were a limited number of works that parodied the current modish prose technique. Pioneered by Remizov, Zamyatin, Bely, and Pilnyak in the twentieth century, this elaborate prose style, termed ornamentalism, was tried by the majority of writers in the first half of the decade. This mass usage reduced the definition of the technique to include any style that called attention to itself in practically any way. The attention was frequently produced by somewhat labored means. Ornamentalism was treated satirically by the aesthetic camp almost exclusively to produce humor. Zoshchenko in *Siren tsvetyot* (*The Lilac is Blooming*) portrays the meeting of two lovers in the woods and then banters with the reader about the method with which such a meeting should be described. This *obnazhenie priyoma* (laying bare the device) effectively contrasts Zoshchenko's style, which calls attention to itself in its own way, with that in vogue at the time:

   Just the same, the author will try to take a dip into highbrow artistic literature.
   The sea gurgled. . . .
   Suddenly, around something there was a curling, scurrying, and prickling.
   It was a young man uncinching his shoulders and cinching his hand into his side pocket.
   In the world there was a bench.
   And so there suddenly entered this world a

ci-
    gar-
        ette,
which
    the
        man
            thoughtfully
                and
s   l   o   w   l   y
caught with his even, dull yellow, slightly protruding teeth (was
it with his teeth?), for this purpose opening his eater a half-
centimeter and twelve millimeters. In doing this, he exposed his
pale red, or rather pink, or more correctly, bluish gums, solidly
bespeckled with teeth, as if with mold. On the upper gum there
was a small (barely visible) dark dot, which hardly glimmered in
the moonlight, and which only the experienced, keen eyes of the
artist could see for the use and glory of our national literature.

The sea gurgled. . . . The grass rustled ceaselessly. The clay
and sand had sifted long before beneath the lovers' feet. The girl
shamblingly and cross-eyedly hatted, hooking the lilac. (The girl
smiled mischievously and merrily, sniffing the lilac.)

Rushya, Rushya, my mother Rushya! Aw, the devil take you!

The sea, that is, I should say, the lake, gurgled, reflected opal
and turquoise, nodded and vomited. Again around something
there was an artistic prickling, scuttling, curling. And suddenly
the colors of the spectrum lit the undulating landscape with their
unutterably wondrous radiance. . . .

Oh, to hell with it! It doesn't come off. The author has the
manliness to confess that he has no gift for so-called highbrow
literature. People have different gifts. The Lord gives one man a
simple rough sort of tongue and another a tongue which can
execute all kinds of subtle artistic ritornellos every minute.[11]

Repetition, infrequently used words, musical terms such as ritornello,
and the use of strange word combinations that seemingly transcend
semantics were exaggerated in such works to parody the style.

The satirical references to individuals often employed ridicule and
sometimes descended to slander. The most frequent individual targets
for the Fellow Traveler and emigré factions of the aesthetic camp were
Mayakovsky and Maxim Gorky. Mayakovsky's brash, bohemian behavior, his propagandistic, frequently subliterary work, and his denunciation of other writers were exposed. The most active contributor to
the satirical image of Mayakovsky was Averchenko, who expressed
emigré dismay at the direction taken by Soviet literature. His treat-

ment of Mayakovsky exhibits the same forcefulness and use of personal references that characterized his treatment of individual Communist leaders. In his sketch *Madam Trotskaya* (*Madame Trotsky*) the regal lady's pompous desire for a court poet precipitates an interview with Mayakovsky: "And so I summoned Mayakovsky. He sat for half an hour, drank half a bottle of cognac, filled all his pockets with cookies, chewed on his fingernails, spit three times on the carpet, and left without excusing himself."[12] Such descriptions came to an abrupt halt in the Soviet Union when Stalin canonized Mayakovsky shortly after the poet committed suicide in 1930.

Averchenko's most forceful jibes were reserved for Gorky, who was endowed with the characteristics of the stereotyped negative Communist and hack writer. In *Maxim Gorky*, Averchenko accuses the acknowledged father of socialist literature of driving many artists and intellectuals abroad and of promoting mediocrity in the rest. The abuse and poverty suffered by those remaining in the Soviet Union are attributed to Gorky, whose humanitarian gestures are viewed as ironically belated and devoid of feeling. The starving artists, scientists, writers, and intellectuals are asked to refer to Gorky as Your Proletarian Majesty, and in return for the pittance of aid, each is asked to write a statement thanking Gorky for his efforts:

> You should give me a testimonial, a reference, in which you
> say this and that, and bequeath to me your heartfelt thanks and
> say that you will never forget so long as you live. And I will frame
> it and hang it on the wall where no one will bother it. It's nothing
> for you to write this, and it pleases me very much.[13]

To Fellow Traveler and especially to emigré satirists Gorky symbolized even more than Mayakovsky the prostitution of literature in both technique and subject matter. Gorky had been proclaimed a saint and was the great authority used to justify pedestrianization. He was the only writer endowed by satirists with political power, and political involvement coupled with a lack of creative ability were the traits most frequently exposed.

The reaction of the political camp to these assaults was usually very direct. In the mass media propagandists and new culturalists defended government controls and attacked the political and literary attitudes of the aesthetic camp. This editorial reaction found its way into literature principally in the work of Mayakovsky. In "The Face of a Class Enemy," "Dayosh tukhlye yaytsa" ("You Give Rotten Eggs"), "Rabot-

nikam stikha i prozy,/Na leto yedushchim v kolkhozy" ("To Poetry and
Prose Workers Going to Collective Farms for the Summer"), and other
short works, Mayakovsky singled out Panteleymon Romanov, Bulgakov, the Korsh Theater, Zamyatin, Pilnyak, Gladkov, Sergey Tret-
yakov, the Moscow Art Theater, and others to receive his criticism for
both ideological shortcomings and literary deviations from the author's
own norm. Bulgakov and Zamyatin were exposed for their satirical
treatment of the new order, Gladkov for his stale and mundanely
ideological prose. It is noteworthy that Mayakovsky did not resort to
exclusively political polemics as one might expect but rather exposed
writers of all political and artistic persuasions. Communists like Gladkov and Romanov were lumped together with heretics like Zamyatin,
and all were proclaimed deviationists for various reasons. Mayakovsky
was prompted by personal bias in addition to ideology and is illustra-
tive of the interfactional polemics and intrafactional disaffection that
were so prevalent.

The political camp also chose targets from the nineteenth and early
twentieth centuries. Many were the same as those exposed by the
aesthetic camp. There was a difference in portrayal, however, as the
political camp emphasized politics more and chose those writers and
literary trends which they felt were most indicative of a bourgeois and
exploitative past. The aesthetic poetic trends that traditionally opposed
the civic movement were often ridiculed. Typical is a stanza from
Bedny's "Strelka" ("The Arrow"):

> Here the subtlest of aesthetes
> Will be whimpering (like before!),
> That the civic type poets
> Are defaming their altar.[14]

His barbs refer to the middle of the nineteenth century, when the
civic-aesthetic controversy in poetry first became significant. But his
concern is also centered on the recent past, on Modernism and its
post-1920 remnants, because it was primarily those poets who condemned Bedny and all that he stood for in poetry.

Mayakovsky exposed the sentimental lyricism of these same aesthetic poets. There is a tragic irony in Mayakovsky's brash denunciation, inasmuch as a significant part of his own poetic output reflected a
hypersensitive lyricism and a sentimentalism based on personal frustration. His satirical references to the literary past were prompted by
his role as propagandist and by a personal contempt for certain poets

and poetic techniques. In "The Bedbug" the author demeans the poetry produced by Prisypkin, the new philistine, by insisting that it resembles that of Alexey Apukhtin and Nadson, two favorites of the socially conscious yet sentimental set at the end of the nineteenth century.[15]

Apart from the polemic on government controls, the major target of the political camp was the literary left. Ornamentalist prose and avant-garde poetic and theatrical trends, including Futurism (despite the alliance with Mayakovsky), were the most frequent targets. The aesthetically conservative proletarian factions produced most of the exposé. Perhaps the most significant target was Vsevolod Meyerhold, whose theatrical experiments were considered bourgeois, formalistic, and incomprehensible to the masses, therefore counterrevolutionary. Meyerhold was also exposed by Ilf and Petrov, who mocked what they considered to be excessive effects. Their references to the eminent director are used for humor. In *The Twelve Chairs*, Gogol's "Zhenitba" ("The Marriage") is presented à la Meyerhold. The result is a virtual circus complete with outlandish costumes, gymnastics, and contemporary political jibes. The viewers understand little and leave confused. Meyerhold was attacked almost exclusively from an aesthetic point of view, and the ideological content of his work was seldom made an issue.

The most significant aspect of the satirical treatment of literature during the decade was the coalition of moderate proregime, Fellow Traveler, and emigré satirists who attacked the party's role in and requirements for literature and the resulting decline in quality. The coalition was by no means formal; it was short lived, and was confined essentially to the theme of literature. It existed because the three factions held, in various degrees, liberal literary views, even though their political postures differed radically. These satirists reacted to issues similarly and exposed the state of literature in the same way. For one of the very few times in the decade the contrast of universality and isolated abuse was ignored, and this harmony of view illustrated the widespread fear and discontent. The coalition is important historically because its fears were realized.

8. The Demise of Satire in the Thirties

THE waning of satire as a result of the first Five-Year Plan developed into its demise with the advent of vigorous government involvement in the arts. Previously the regime had been content to assume a general guardianship while permitting various factions to exist and to compete among themselves for literary dominance. Trotsky's statement that "Our policy in art, during a transitional period, can and must be to help the various groups and schools of art which have come over to the Revolution to grasp correctly the historic meaning of the Revolution, and to allow them complete freedom of self-determination in the field of art, after putting before them the categorical standard of being for or against the Revolution" guided government policy generally during the twenties despite his personal conflicts with other government ideologists and the clear official preference for some kind of a new revolutionary proletarian culture.[1] Literary purges, such as those endured by Zamyatin and Pilnyak, and politico-literary infighting among the various proletarian groups resulted from such a generous policy, however, and it finally became necessary from the government's perspective to adopt more forceful measures. Thus in 1932 by a resolution of the Central Committee all literary factions were formally disbanded and placed into a single Union of Soviet Writers.

The creation of the Union of Soviet Writers had an immediate deleterious effect on the fragile balance between proregime and antiregime camps. A single organization eliminated the entire concept of a Fellow Traveler as one who was in the Revolution but not of it. The decision also eliminated much of the satirical dialogue among factions and restricted not only the number of satirical targets but also the manner and intensity with which they could be exposed. It was clear that the intent was to create a unified literary voice and a mechanism to guarantee that the voice spoke accurately and on cue. These guidelines developed logically from the mustering of forces characteristic of the

129

first Five-Year Plan, and the satire that was written by the majority of writers in 1932–33 differed little from that produced in the late twenties. Satire might have actively continued, albeit in a muffled voice, had the only constraint been the Union of Soviet Writers in its infant stage. Satire often prospers under strictures and perhaps even requires them, but the choral voice that the regime required and the procedures used to achieve it in this instance threatened to make satire an obsolete mode of expression.

The two largest barriers to satire's continued existence were the institution of Socialist Realism as the proper method in fiction and the purges of heretics of all persuasions, including literary ones, in the remaining years of the decade. Socialist Realism was formally spawned in 1934 at the First Congress of Soviet Writers at which Andrey Zhdanov, a career party functionary with little literary expertise or sensitivity, spoke for the government:

> In our country the chief heroes of literary works are the active builders of a new life: working men and women, collective farmers, engineers, members of the Komsomol, pioneers. . . . Our literature is saturated with enthusiasm and heroism. It is optimistic, but not through any zoological instinct. It is fundamentally optimistic, because it is the literature of the rising class of proletariat, the only progressive and advanced class.
>
> Comrade Stalin described our writers as engineers of human minds. What does it mean? What does this title impose upon you?
>
> It means, above all, to know life in order to depict it truthfully in works of art, to depict it not scholastically, not lifelessly, not just as "objective reality," but to depict real life in its revolutionary development.
>
> In so doing, truthfulness and historical concreteness of artistic depiction must be combined with the task of ideological remolding and re-education of the toiling people in the spirit of Socialism. This method in fiction and in literary criticism is what we call Socialist Realism. . . .[2]

A satirist could clearly work within these boundaries were it not for the accuracy of Zamyatin's view of the implementation procedures expressed earlier in *We*, that as the United State moved toward a contemporary reality, literature fell into the bland sameness that nearly destroyed it.

If the requirement for ideology had once been onerous, it became even more so after 1934. The infusion of canonized principles into works of humor and satire by a writer who generally looks for flaws and discrepancies emerges as a literary anomaly. The literary and political recipe was foreign to the taste of many, yet official circumstances precluded the humorous objections of the twenties. Zoshchenko's earlier objection to ideological strictures was made to sound out of place and even dangerous in the middle thirties:

> . . .being a writer is sort of hard. . . . Take ideology—these days a writer has got to have ideology.
> Here's Voronsky now (a good man) who writes: "It is necessary that writers should have a more precise ideology."
> Now that's plumb disagreeable! Tell me, how can I have a "precise ideology" when not a single party among them all appeals to me?
> I don't hate anybody—that's *my* precise ideology. . . .
> In their general swing the Bolsheviks are closer to me than anybody else. And so I'm willing to bolshevik around with them. . . . But I'm not a Communist (or rather a Marxist), and I think I never shall be.[3]

While Zoshchenko's sentiments may never have changed, his external performance did; in the thirties he turned to longer forms to produce several collections of stories, in effect abandoning the satirical sketch which had made him the most popular of the satirists a decade earlier.

Zoshchenko's retreat was judicious, as even the stalwarts of agitprop found reason for concern in the era of the purges. Demyan Bedny, whose orthodoxy in attacking approved targets since the Revolution had never really been questioned, was purged from the party and found it difficult to publish anywhere. It is ironic that a writer who had penned over 250,000 lines and whose 204 books had been published in 12 million copies should suddenly find that he was unacceptable to officialdom.[4] Yet his dogmatic statements about art had an unfamiliar ring in an era in which the government preferred to speak for itself in all matters. In this regard Bedny might well share the sentiments of Olesha, whose speech at the First Congress of Soviet Writers expressed sincere distress that what he had valued in the past was somehow no longer valid.

In the early thirties the thematics of the twenties remained largely intact, with predictable changes of emphasis dictated by the political and literary climate. The theme of the Revolution and the attendant themes of the Civil War, the White, and the Communist were no longer prominent, but periodic references were made to the practical effect of the Revolution upon the people. Fellow Travelers had always insisted that the common people poorly understood October, that they were motivated more by their own immediate interests than by any abstract principle (as demonstrated in Zamyatin's *Ex* and Bulgakov's *Heart of a Dog*), and that they quickly reverted to their prerevolutionary thoughts, feelings, and actions. Zamyatin continued these themes with *Lev* (*The Lion*) published in emigration in 1935. The young hero volunteers for the part of a lion in a spectacle. His role consists of allowing the heroine to stab him with a spear; then he plunges to his theatrical death over a makeshift cliff. Reminiscent of the role of "Marfism" in *Ex*, the would-be actor seeks the role because of Katya, an emancipated Soviet woman in whom he is interested. She insists that women now have the same rights as men, that they can indulge in free love, and that marriage means nothing. Her interest in performers prompts his seeking the part of the lion. When, however, it comes time for him to fall, he is afraid and hesitates:

> In the front rows the voice of the director could be heard screeching in a terrible whisper: "Jump, you devil, jump!" And then all saw something absolutely fantastic: the lion raised his right paw, quickly crossed himself, and then like a rock plunged over the cliff.[5]

The remnants of religion in the mid-thirties were more serious than in the twenties, and through them Zamyatin shows that no substantive changes had occurred because of October.

Consumer problems and the issues of contemporary life, highlighted during the NEP years, continued to appear in the early thirties in the works of those satirists who had written about them a decade earlier. Zoshchenko's comic story *Baths and People* is a follow-up to his *The Bathhouse*. In the story, reminiscent of his humorous sketch form, Zoshchenko recalls the past problem and notes that the Bath and Laundry Trust has taken strong action but that the bath patrons still have no place to put their locker keys and tags. The theme of poverty, common in the twenties, is emphasized through another popular theme, theft. While people are bathing, clothes are stolen from lockers, but all that is obtained are virtual rags. The story could easily have been written a decade earlier; it shows that the changes in Zoshchenko's art in the thirties were externally motivated and did not result from a decreased sense of art.

Bulgakov, in his satirical masterpiece *The Master and Margarita*, also treats the themes of contemporary life and the economy. The novel was written secretly during the thirties and is the most important work of satire of its time. One must wait for the emergence of Andrey Sinyavsky in 1959 before a satirist of such import dares to write again. *The Master and Margarita* shows that the Soviet economy still lags and that Muscovites have not changed appreciably from their bourgeois ancestors. The magician Voland, who is Satan incarnate, offers those who attend his magic show money and the newest Parisian fashions in exchange for their old clothes. There is a chaotic scramble for the bills, which are later transformed into labels and illegal foreign currency, and for the clothing, which vanishes, thereby creating a shocking burlesque. Muscovites clamor for such items not only because of the deficiency of the Soviet economy but also because of their bourgeois natures. The consumer failures of the economy are aggravated by the operation of special stores at which only foreign currency is accepted. The fact that certain Soviet officials are able to use these stores, pretending at the same time to be foreigners, only amplifies the picture of economic discrimination, social priorities, and official favoritism that tends to gratify hidden bourgeois desires at the highest levels.

Although after 1930 he came to derive much of the material for his stories and sketches from visits to construction sites, factories, and collective farms, Valentin Kataev also portrayed the bourgeois Communist, an outgrowth of NEP that endured into the thirties. "Doroga tsvetov" ("A Flowery Road"), a play reminiscent of his earlier play "Squaring the Circle," depicts a contemporary type named Zavyalov who continually lectures on the golden horizon of socialism and on the man of the future. The verbiage translates into some very personal meanings for him, however, such as free love, abolishing the institution of marriage, and absolute individual freedom. He pursues this life style but loses his family and the women who share his ideas for a time, and he finally settles for a solitary life in a small, windowless room. Kataev dutifully punishes his hero and clearly shows that he is an exception to the norm and that his ideology is destined to fail. Bulgakov, on the contrary, not only generalizes his assertions but insists on a lack of repentance and retribution.

Bulgakov also resurrected the spectre of the housing crisis as part of his reevaluation of the problems of contemporary life. As before the satiric barbs fell upon the overcrowded conditions and upon the figure of the chairman of the local housing committee. In *The Master and Margarita*, Nikanor Bosoy, the housing official, is besieged following the death of Berlioz by tenants requesting that they be allotted his living space. Space is at such a premium that the requests carry an aura of desperation:

> They contained entreaties, threats, intrigue, denunciations, promises to redecorate the apartment at personal expense, remarks about intolerable overcrowding and the impossibility of sharing an apartment with hoodlums. Among them was a description, shattering in its literary power, of the theft of some meatballs from someone's jacket pocket in apartment No. 31, two promises of suicide and one confession of secret pregnancy.[6]

Berlioz's death also brings his uncle Poplavsky madly scurrying from the country to Moscow in hope of securing his late nephew's apartment for himself. Thus, despite promises, threats, and exposure, the crisis abides in unsolved major proportions. It is also noteworthy that Bosoy in a moment of contrition admits that all who serve on the housing committee are thieves, thereby validating the postrevolutionary opinion of many and the satirical depiction of the situation. The fact that Margarita's husband has a large five-room apartment envied by tens of thousands of Muscovites serves to accentuate the problem and recalls the earlier portrayal of the prosperous condition of the new Communist aristocrats.

The theme of religion developed somewhat differently in the thirties. Bedny continued to depict the village priest and the superstitions of the common people but added comments about the Pope and German persecution of the Jews, inasmuch as political conditions dictated several allusions to foreign governments. Bulgakov belittled this official campaign against religion by depicting the editor Berlioz in *The Master and Margarita* commissioning an antireligious poem from the poet Bezdomny. Bezdomny's work is a failure because, even though he endowed Christ with every possible flaw and vice, he portrayed him as a living historical figure. Berlioz, consistent with official preference, had wanted to deny the existence completely. The most significant development in the theme of religion was the more detailed picture of American religion provided by Ilf and Petrov's *Odnoetazhnaya Amerika* (*Single-storied America*, in the English edition translated as *Little Golden America*). The book was the outgrowth of a 1935–36 tour of America that the writers undertook as official correspondents of *Pravda*; it provided a critically well received picture of America.

With the exception of Zamyatin's *A Fisher of Men* and Ehrenburg's portrayal of Mr. Cool there had been little attention paid to the Western church. Ilf and Petrov provide specific humorous and satirical details to a subject that was fast becoming passé because of the political situation. Of particular satirical interest was American fundamentalism as found in the Salvation Army and the Baptist Church. The authors portray a Salvation Army hostel in New York that compares favorably with the filth and degradation found in Gorky's "Na dne" ("The Lower Depths"). An old man harangues the hostel's residents while standing in front of a backdrop of the American flag and placards of Biblical quotations. He announces that he has turned to God and challenges others to use his life as an example:

He had been a bum ("the same kind of a miserable bum that you are, you old devils!"), he led a disgusting life, blasphemed ("remember your habits, my friends!"), thieved—yes, all of this, unfortunately, happened. Now all this is over. He now has his own home; he lives like a respectable person ("God created us in His image and after His likeness, didn't He?"). Recently he even bought himself a radio. And all of this he acquired directly with God's help. [7]

The same orientation is found in California, where the travelers pick up a young Baptist hitchhiker who promptly informs them that all of Russia will perish at the imminent Second Coming. His pastor has taught him that the Second Coming will undoubtedly occur in two or three years and that Russians will perish because they are unbelievers. Western religion is thus portrayed as an illogical system of absolutes, but it is not linked with the government as was the portrayal of the new official religion following the Revolution.

Ilf and Petrov significantly advanced the stereotype of the West and in the process used many details and concepts that were popular in the twenties. The picture of America as a nation valuing money above all else, indulging in debauchery, and opposing the labor movement had already been established by Ehrenburg and Tolstoy. Ilf and Petrov reemphasize that money is the real moving force in American life and show its influence from various perspectives. The

din of New York speaks in terms of money: "Evening New York in all of
its facets speaks to those who stroll the streets: Give a nickel, drop in a
nickel! Part with your nickel and you will be happy!"[8] Big money
interests dominate life: "the banks will swallow him up. It always ends
that way in America."[9] Financiers and industrialists such as J. P.
Morgan and Henry Ford despise and try to destroy one another. City
slums with rampant crime, pervasive filth, and a worker population
exist in proximity to the estates and businesses of regal American
capitalists:

> Some Communist Party workers live on two dollars per week,
> an amusing figure for a nation of millionaires. But despite this
> they struggle bravely with their pitiable crumbs against the likes
> of Morgan. . . . And they are successful. Morgan and others like
> him with their billions and their powerful press are afraid of them
> and hate them.[10]

The themes of power, persecution, and the press are intimately connected with the practical religion of capitalism, and the satirists show
that money and the abuse of money violate the norms of human
conduct. The mythic capitalists of Tolstoy and Ehrenburg are transformed into the reality of Ford and Morgan, but the results are largely
the same.

Money is also inseparably linked with Hollywood, which continues
to function according to the principles of financial empires as portrayed
in Ehrenburg's *The Dream Factory*. Bankers and other financial figures as negative personages disappear from movies and are portrayed
only as devoted practitioners of good will who help the poor and young
people in love. This results from the fact that huge financial interests
have come to control Hollywood. A by-product of financial control,
according to Ilf and Petrov, has been the destruction of the film as an
art form and its transformation into a profitable venture akin to the
selling of balloons. The authors report the opinion of a Hollywood
functionary to the effect that:

> It is not by chance that we make idiotic films. We are ordered
> to make them. They make them on purpose. Hollywood is inten-
> tionally stuffing Americans' heads with nonsense, stupefying
> them with their films. A Hollywood film will not treat a single
> serious question of life. . . . Our bosses won't permit it. . . .
> They have taught the American viewer not to think.[11]

The only Hollywood cliché not emphasized by Ilf and Petrov is the debauchery attributed to movies and movie life. To compensate, moral decay is generalized into society at large through the depiction of burlesques. The scene is New York, the symbol of most of what is wrong with America. The authors visit a burlesque where they watch several women in turn perform their trade: "They sang with no voice and no sense of music and danced with the dexterity of a kangaroo."[12] The same comic picture is portrayed in *Kolumb prichalivaet k beregu* (*Columbus Lands on the Shore*), a short story written concurrently with their travel notes. In the sketch the mystified Columbus attempts to describe the strange spectacle of burlesque:

> I was impressed by one ritual which takes place every evening in the place called Broadway. A large crowd of natives gathers in a large hut called a burlesque. Several native girls in turn walk up on the stage and to the barbaric din of tom-toms and saxophones gradually take their clothes off. Those present clap feverishly like children. When the girl is almost totally naked and the natives in the hall are heated up to the fullest extent, there occurs something incomprehensible in this ritual: the curtain for some reason or other is lowered and all go home to their huts.[13]

American morality, or lack thereof, is portrayed with humor, and the image is not the same as that of Paris and France generally as found in the works of Ehrenburg and Tolstoy. Burlesques are a comment on American life in a minor key, and the topic does not generate the same satirical intensity as does the theme of money and the figure of the capitalist.

The American labor movement and its attendant themes of police brutality and government repression remained a subject of some rancor in the thirties. Bedny continued to write verse exposing the conflict between the police and workers and made specific references to such topics as alleged abuse at Ford plants. As the political climate in the thirties worsened, such references became more common. In *Single-storied America*, Ilf and Petrov portray the Ford plant in Dearborn, Michigan, at which the workers eat sitting on cement despite Ford's professions of being the friend of the working man. The writers also unleash the theme of police brutality and do so through the feelings of a young man who has become a Communist because of his disaffection with the capitalist system and who combats the exploitation of Mexican and Filipino workers in America. He paints a dismal and indicting picture:

We have already lost several dead, but we will struggle to the
end. . . . Last night the police tried to bring in strikebreakers to
the ships. They began to move in around our pickets and to use
revolvers. . . . Many workers were threatened with arrest.[14]

The portrayal of the Western police and their antipathy to the worker is
reminiscent of the depiction of the White shortly after the Revolution:
they are typically faceless and are characterized by what they do. They
are not individuals but are viewed as a mass threat. Ilf and Petrov do
single out an individual but it is only to use him to indict the system he
serves. Reminiscent of Ehrenburg's sarcastic reference to Sing Sing
Prison in *The Dream Factory*, the authors take a personal tour of the
facility but permit one of the employees of the prison to be their satiric
voice. After conducting the writers to the electric chair, he observes
that he understands that the Soviet penal system is designed to re-
habilitate the criminal while the American system is intended only to
punish. Such sentiments from a non-Soviet significantly enhance the
satiric impact.

Ilf and Petrov also further developed the theme of racism, a rather
minor theme in the twenties even in the work of agitprop satirists.
Previously references to racism were infrequent, poorly developed,
and very topical, but the authors' journey through the southern states
in 1935–36 stimulates some caustic comments, heretofore almost
nonexistent in prose:

Negroes are talented. At any rate Whites willingly applaud
them while continuing to consider them a lower race. Negroes
are benevolently permitted to become performers. Obviously,
when a Black is on stage and a White is sitting in a theater box, he
can look down on the Black and his master's pride does not suffer.
Negroes are impressionable. Whites relate to this ironically
and consider Negroes stupid. Indeed! One does not need to be
impressionable in order to trade well. . . .
Negroes have almost been denied the opportunity to grow and
develop. In the cities the only careers open to them are as porters
and elevator boys, while in their home land in the Southern
States they are disenfranchised hired hands who have been lowered to the condition of domestic animals—here they are
slaves.[15]

This response to the theme was rather isolated, and the topic of racism was not important during the years of internal political turmoil and the threat of war with Germany.

Germany itself, a rather minor satirical target earlier compared with France, England, and America, gained significance with the rise of Fascism. Bedny and other agitprop satirists used frequent topical allusions to Hitler and Heinrich Himmler, the chief of the Gestapo, and to Fascism as an idea. In fact the satiric treatment of foreign lands and peoples, with the important exception of *Single-storied America*, was largely confined to a militant unmasking of German politics. In order to lend credence to the satirical onslaught satirists often combined official enemies into a single target, and during the decade Trotsky and his attendant heresies were identified with Fascism. He is portrayed as a Judas whose allegiance is to Fascism, not to the Revolution.

One would presume that the rapid pedestrianization of the arts in the thirties and the obvious theoretical and practical threats to satire would produce a satirical response to the conditions and underground tactics designed to circumvent strictures. Because of the severe political conditions strong literary objections were not forthcoming, but several writers, including such giants as Pasternak and Bulgakov, began to write for their own sealed drawers. The satirical response to the literary world of the day was confined almost exclusively to Bulgakov's *The Master and Margarita*, whose satirical barbs were sheathed for over twenty years before they could be loosed.

Bulgakov took direct aim at the quality of Soviet literature, at privilege, and at the way quality was defined. The poet Bezdomny, whose antireligous poem is rejected for its historicity, vows never to write his terrible poetry again after he meets the Master. Ryukhin, a poet whom Bezdomny meets in the psychiatric ward, comes to acknowledge that he does not believe in any of the proletarian slogans he writes. Poetry declined in the years following the Civil War, and much of what was written was produced by proletarian and agitprop writers who were interested in building the new system and who used a rather fixed system of clichés and attitudes. By showing that two poets determine to abandon their pseudocraft, that the Master is ruined by a rigid Soviet critic, and that he finds peace with his manuscript only in a state of supernatural rest provided by Voland, Bulgakov demonstrates his caustic attitude toward the state of the arts. His feelings about art are understandably more negative than they were in the late twenties, when he mocked the censorship mechanism, reflecting his private struggles with official censorship and literary theory.

Bulgakov also attacks the privileges afforded orthodox writers and the caste system that is prevalent in the literary organizations and by extension in the Union of Soviet Writers. The vehicle in *The Master and Margarita* for his satiric antagonism is the Griboedov House, the home of MASSOLIT, one of Moscow's largest and most prestigious literary clubs. The house is so named because it was possibly owned by the aunt of the poet and playwright, and it provides a most tenuous link between the political elitism and literary boorishness of contemporary writers and the sophisticated dedication to art characteristic of Alexander Griboedov. The members of the club live very well, far better than the average (and even not so average) citizen, and their membership cards are the envy of all. The exclusiveness of the club, as ensured by the cards, remains intact until challenged by Voland's retinue. Koroviev and Begemot seek admission but are refused because they do not possess the marvelous document. They object that a writer is not defined in terms of a document but in terms of what he writes and note that

> To prove to yourself that Dostoevsky is a writer, would you really ask him for his membership card? Just take any five pages from any of his novels and you won't need a membership card to convince yourself that you are dealing with a real writer.[16]

The retinue is finally admitted not because of their arguments but because they are recognized as participants in the recent mysterious happenings in Moscow and as possessors of potentially harmful power. Ironically Koroviev and Begemot promptly identify themselves as Panaev and Skabichevsky, two representatives of a liberal, socially conscious, nineteenth-century group of writers and critics, a group whose views were not consonant with the directions adopted by Socialist Realism. Once the supernatural visitors are inside, a scandalous row predictably ensues that results in a fire that destroys the building. The destruction of the literary past is a metaphor for what has already taken place, and thus one cannot regret too deeply the destruction of what MASSOLIT means in the present. To amplify this, Voland wryly comments that he hopes that the new house will be better. Since Voland is the one who symbolically rescues literature in the person of the Master, it is appropriate that he voices hope for Russia's literary future.

The other major satirical treatment of literature in the thirties is Bulgakov's *A Theatrical Novel*, usually rendered in English as *Black*

Snow. The novel is a semiautobiographical work stemming from Bulgakov's request that the regime attach him to the Moscow Art Theater in any capacity. The request, stimulated by the removal of his "Days of the Turbins" from the repertoire and official ostracism of his other dramatic work, was granted, and this provided a living wage and a certain insulation from the Stalinist purges. His split with Stanislavsky, initiated as early as 1932 when Bulgakov refused to rewrite passages of his "Molière" to mask allusions to Stalin and Stalinism, became final in 1936, whereupon he assumed a position as a librettist for the Bolshoy Theater. These turbulent years with Stanislavsky were punctuated with frequent literary disagreements, and the experience provides much of the basis of *A Theatrical Novel*. Subjects which had been common satirical targets in the twenties, such as currying favor with important bureaucrats by supplying them with complimentary theater tickets, were resurrected by Bulgakov in the novel, and indeed he is the most important voice in Soviet satire in matters respecting the theater. Mostly his spleen is vented on the person of Ivan Vasilievich, the analogue of Stanislavsky, whom satire spared and whom theater people generally respected. Bulgakov presents quite another picture:

> His charm is revealed as no more than a tool with which to manipulate people, his dedication is unmasked as the purest egomania, his fostering of artistic talent as sheer favouritism; his famous "method" has ossified into a set of idiosyncratic mannerisms deeply inimical to any spark of original talent. The harmony and unity which outwardly characterized the MAT [Moscow Art Theater] is debunked as largely a sham. Riven vertically between the Stanislavsky devotees on one side and the protégés of Nemirovich-Danchenko (the latter included Bulgakov himself) on the other, there is an equally yawning horizontal gulf between the aspiring younger generation of actors and old stagers who are fiercely determined to go on hogging all the good parts.[17]

Other satirical themes that were common during the flourishing of satire are rare in the thirties. Bulgakov raised the spectre of the all-powerful document in *The Master and Margarita* by noting that if one removes a person's documents from existence, he also removes the person. One individual who spends an evening at Satan's ball even demands a document authenticating his whereabouts in order to avoid problems with the police and his wife. In the same novel Bulgakov again exposes the Soviet penchant for finding someone to blame, a scapegoat to remove official obligation and responsibility. After Voland's retinue leaves Moscow, there are several arrests, numerous self-serving official explanations, and many black cats killed as a consequence of the activities of Begemot, a feline member of Voland's group the size of a large pig.

In the thirties, Bedny continued to pen verse that attacked the infamous Whites of a decade earlier, and there were periodic allusions to Yudenich and Wrangel. But generally the themes associated with the Revolution and contemporary life are missing because of Socialist Realism and the difficult political situation. It must be remembered that these themes dominated satire at its apex, and when they became passé, satire diminished. When the existence of two literary camps was denied by the creation of the writers' union and when the tenor of literature became more somber and utilitarian, the demise of satire was largely complete. The faint embers that remained sparked only infrequently and ineffectually, and the satirical mode assumed a monotonous tone that has overshadowed efforts to revitalize it.

Notes

1. THE BACKGROUND

1. A. N. Starkov, *Voprosy teorii sovetskogo satiricheskogo feletona v kritike dvadtsatykh godov* [*Questions of the Theory of the Soviet Satirical Feuilleton in the Criticism of the 1920's*], pp. 479–80.

2. Ilya Ehrenburg, *Neobychaynye pokhozhdenia Khulio Khurenito* [*The Extraordinary Adventures of Julio Jurenito*].

3. L. F. Yershov, *Sovetskaya satiricheskaya proza* [*Soviet Satirical Prose*], p. 56.

4. In the words of Alvin B. Kernan, *The Plot of Satire*: "The use of type characters is, of course, common in satire, for the satirist is never interested in deep explorations of human nature. His characters are merely personifications of the particular form of dullness he wishes to give visible shape" (p. 149).

5. Edward J. Brown, *Russian Literature since the Revolution*, p. 231.

6. Kernan, pp. 171–72.

7. Leonard Feinberg, *The Satirist: His Temperament, Motivation, and Influence*, p. 302.

8. Robert C. Elliott, *The Power of Satire: Magic, Ritual, Art*, p. 265.

9. Feinberg, p. 308. Saltykov's Aesopian language may be seen as a result of this phenomenon.

10. Marc Slonim, *Soviet Russian Literature: Writers and Problems*, pp. 53–54.

11. Hugh McLean, "On the Style of the Leskovian Skaz," p. 299.

12. Valentin Kataev, *Sobranie sochineny v devyati tomakh* [*Collected Works in Nine Volumes*], 2:618.

13. Maxim Gorky, *Sobranie sochineny v tridtsati tomakh* [*Collected Works in Thirty Volumes*], 24:262.

14. Yershov, p. 184.

15. Ibid., p. 200.

16. Ibid., p. 207.

2. THE REVOLUTION AND THE CIVIL WAR: EVENT AND EFFECT

1. Yevgeny Zamyatin, *Sobranie sochineny* [*Collected Works*], 3:7.

2. Ibid., 3:8.

3. Ibid., 3:270.

4. Ibid., 3:288–89.

5. Ibid., 3:315.

6. Yevgeny Zamyatin, *My* [*We*], p. 5.

7. Ibid., p. 100.

8. Zamyatin, *Collected Works*, 3:65.

9. Zamyatin, *We*, p. 14.

10. Alexey Remizov, *Vzvikhryonnaya Rus* [*Turbulent Russia*], p. 191, *V rozovom bleske* [*On a Field Azure*], p. 245. A more literal translation of the latter title is *In a Rosy Light*.

11. Ivan Shmelyov, *Pro odnu starukhu: Novye rasskazy o Rossii* [*About an Old Woman: New Stories about Russia*], p. 168.

12. Arkady Averchenko, *Dyuzhina nozhey v spinu revolyutsii: 12 novykh rasskazov* [*A Dozen Knives in the Revolution's Back: Twelve New Stories*], p. 6. The acronyms cited by Averchenko are equivalent to the following: *Sovnarkhoz* (Council of the National Economy), *Uezemelkom* (Regional Land Commission), *Sovbur* (Soviet Labor Camp Barracks or Soviet Fortified Coastal Region), *Revvoenkom* (Revolutionary Military Committee).

13. Olga Gromov Sorokin, "Ivan Šmelëv: His Life and Work," p. 87.

14. Ivan Shmelyov, *Solntse myortvykh* [*The Sun of the Dead*], p. 39.

15. N. A. Teffi, *Rys* [*At a Trot*], pp. 128, 129.

16. Valentin Kataev, *Borodaty malyutka: Yumoristicheskie rasskazy* [*The Bearded Baby: Humorous Stories*], p. 42.

17. Zamyatin, *Collected Works*, 4:182–83.

18. Mikhail Zoshchenko, *Nervnye lyudi* [*Nervous People*], pp. 67, 68.

19. Remizov, *Turbulent Russia*, p. 164.

20. Kataev, *The Bearded Baby*, p. 28.

21. Gleb Struve, *Soviet Russian Literature 1917–1950*.

22. Mikhail Bulgakov, *Sbornik rasskazov* [*A Collection of Stories*], p. 179.

23. Demyan Bedny, *Sobranie sochineny v vosmi tomakh* [*Collected Works in Eight Volumes*], 4:85.

24. Kataev, *Collected Works in Nine Volumes*, 2:558.

25. Ibid., 2:564.

26. Arkady Averchenko, *Nechistaya sila: Kniga novykh rasskazov* [*An Unclean Power: A Book of New Stories*], p. 8.

27. Bedny, 4:100.

28. Ibid., 4:227.

29. Vladimir Mayakovsky, *Sobranie sochineny v vosmi tomakh* [*Collected Works in Eight Volumes*], 2:324.

30. A. M. van der Eng–Liedmeier, *Soviet Literary Characters: An Investigation into the Portrayal of Soviet Men in Russian Prose 1917–1953*, p. 20.

31. Zamyatin, *Collected Works*, 3:217.

32. Vyacheslav Zavalishin, *Early Soviet Writers*, p. 331.

33. van der Eng–Liedmeier, pp. 21–22.

34. Shmelyov, *About an Old Woman*, p. 36.

35. Ehrenburg, *The Extraordinary Adventures of Julio Jurenito*, p. 36.

36. Zamyatin, *Collected Works*, 3:225.

37. Ibid., 4:147.

38. Averchenko, *A Dozen Knives in the Revolution's Back*, pp. 34–35.

39. Arkady Averchenko, *Razvorochenny muraveynik: Emigrantskie rasskazy* [*The Toppled Anthill: Emigré Stories*], p. 228.

40. Ibid., p. 230. The original ironically refers to Bela Kun as Bela Kum, thereby connoting an old gossip.

3. THE EMIGRÉ

1. Nikolay Berdyaev (1874–1948) was a popular Russian philosopher who turned from Marxism to Idealism and ultimately to Orthodox Christianity. He opposed the Bolsheviks from the point of view of personal freedom and was expelled from the

Soviet Union in 1922. Dmitry Merezhkovsky (1865–1941) was an early Symbolist poet and philosopher who strongly objected to collectivism and who lived abroad after 1917.

2. Rudolph Steiner (1861–1925) was an Austrian philosopher whose theory of anthroposophy influenced Andrey Bely's novel *Kotik Letaev*. The philosophy proposes an elevated spiritual world that is accessible to man's higher faculties.

3. Arkady Averchenko, *Yumoristicheskie rasskazy* [*Humorous Stories*], p. 271.

4. A. N. Tolstoy, *Polnoe sobranie sochineny* [*Complete Collected Works*], 4:330.

5. Ehrenburg appears to have contrived both the figure of Blagoverov and his journal *The Russian Fire-Alarm*, the name of which transmits its muckraking intent. Milyukov, the foreign minister in the Provisional Government, is cited most likely to give credibility to the exposé, since he became one of the most renowned emigré journalists. The journal *Voice of Freedom* also appears to be fictitious but could be a reference to Milyukov's famous Parisian daily *Poslednie novosti* (*The Latest News*).

4. CONTEMPORARY LIFE

1. Mikhail Zoshchenko, *Nad kem smeyotes* [*Who Are You Laughing At?*], pp. 103, 104.

2. Averchenko, *The Toppled Anthill: Emigré Stories*, p. 67.

3. Kataev, *The Bearded Baby: Humorous Stories*, pp. 87–88.

4. Mikhail Bulgakov, *Sobachie serdtse* [*Heart of a Dog*], pp. 13, 17.

5. Zoshchenko, *Who Are You Laughing At?*, p. 79.

6. Averchenko, *Dvenadtsat portretov* [*Twelve Portraits*], p. 78. The acronyms are equivalent to the following: *Derkombed* (Rural Commission on Poverty), *Uezemelkom* (Regional Land Commission), *Gubsovnarkhoz* (Provincial Council of the National Economy), *Osotop* (Fuel Production Industry), *Vseobuch* (Universal Primary Education).

7. Platonov, *Izbrannoe* [*Selected Works*], p. 144.

8. Compare the image of officialdom in such works as Saltykov's *Gubernskie ocherki* (*Provincial Sketches*), *Pompadury i pompadurshi* (*Pompadours and Pompadouresses*), and *Gospoda Tashkenttsy* (*Gentlemen of Tashkent*), Leskov's *Ocharovanny strannik* (*The Enchanted Wanderer*), and *Zayachy remiz* (*Hare Park*), Alexander Ostrovsky's "Dokhodnoe mesto" ("A Good Post"), Alexander Sukhovo-Kobylin's "Delo" ("The Affair"), Turgenev's *Kontora* (*The Office*), and Chekhov's *Moya zhizn* (*My Life*).

9. Bulgakov, *A Collection of Stories*, p. 181.

10. In the words of L. F. Yershov, "*The Embezzlers* was the first satirical tale which enjoyed significant success at the time it was written. Critics noted it and readers loved it; it was staged at the Moscow Art Theater" (*Soviet Satirical Prose*, p. 74).

11. Valentin Kataev, *Sobranie sochineny v pyati tomakh* [*Collected Works in Five Volumes*], 1:66.

12. Platonov, *Selected Works*, pp. 138, 163.

13. Kataev, *Collected Works in Five Volumes*, 4:210.

14. Mikhail Bulgakov, *Dramy i komedii* [*Dramas and Comedies*], p. 197.

15. Kataev, *The Bearded Baby: Humorous Stories*, p. 32

16. Ibid., p. 36.

17. Vladimir Mayakovsky, *Satira* [*Satire*], p. 31.

5. FOREIGN LANDS AND PEOPLES

1. Zamyatin, *Collected Works*, 3:16.

2. Kiparsky, *English and American Characters in Russian Fiction*, p. 51.

3. Yury Olesha, *Pesy* [*Plays*], p. 134.

4. Mayakovsky, *Collected Works in Eight Volumes*, 8:62.
5. Ilya Ehrenburg, *Sobranie sochineny v devyati tomakh* [*Collected Works in Nine Volumes*], 1:239.
6. Ilya Ehrenburg, *Fabrika snov: khronika nashego vremeni* [*The Dream Factory: A Chronicle of Our Time*], p. 95.
7. Tolstoy, *Complete Collected Works*, 5:8.
8. Mayakovsky, *Satire*, p. 49.
9. Mayakovsky, *Collected Works in Eight Volumes*, 4:469.

6. RELIGIOUS AND OTHER MALEFACTORS

1. V. Ruzhina, *Mayakovsky protiv religii* [*Mayakovsky against Religion*], p. 112.
2. Zoshchenko, *Nervous People*, p. 91.
3. Mayakovsky, *Collected Works in Eight Volumes*, 3:314–15.
4. Mikhail Zoshchenko, *Povesti i rasskazy* [*Tales and Stories*], p. 62.
5. Zoshchenko, *Nervous People*, p. 51.

7. LITERATURE

1. Don-Aminado, *Nasha malenkaya zhizn* [*Our Small Life*], p. 141.
2. Zamyatin, *Collected Works*, 3:284.
3. Zamyatin, *We*, pp. 59–60.
4. Ibid., p. 61.
5. Ehrenburg, *The Stormy Life of Laz Roitshvantz*, p. 81.
6. Ehrenburg, *Collected Works in Nine Volumes*, 2:60.
7. Don-Aminado, *Our Small Life*, p. 178.
8. The Russian is "U lukomorya dub zelyony;/Zlataya tsep na dube tom;/I dnyom i nochyu kot uchyony/Vsyo khodit po tsepi krugom."
9. Don-Aminado, *Our Small Life*, p. 182. The Russian reads: "U Baltmorbazy yasen krasny,/Stalnaya tsep lezhit na yom;/Vosmichasovy trud prekrasny,/A, kstati, koshka ne pri chyom."
10. Alexander Blok (1880–1921) was an intensely personal poet and perhaps the most renowned figure of Symbolism. Semyon Nadson (1862–87), idealistic and socially conscious, exemplified the civic trend in poetry. Afanasy Fet (1820–92) was an aesthetic poet whose metaphysical poetry late in his career made him a precursor of Symbolism. The Superfluous Man is a character type out of the nineteenth century who, despite his lofty rhetoric, is unable to accomplish anything practical, fails in love, and does not find a useful role for himself in society.
11. Mikhail Zoshchenko, *Nervous People and Other Satires*, pp. 45–47.
12. Averchenko, *Twelve Portraits*, p. 13.
13. Ibid., p. 29.
14. Bedny, *Collected Works in Eight Volumes*, 4:118.
15. Alexey Apukhtin (1841–93) was a minor poet whose verse expressed nostalgia for lost youth and its pleasures.

8. THE DEMISE OF SATIRE IN THE THIRTIES

1. Leon Trotsky, *Literature and Revolution*, p. 14.
2. Gleb Struve, *Russian Literature under Lenin and Stalin 1917–1953*, p. 262.
3. Ibid., p. 54. Alexander Voronsky (1884–1937) was a moderate Marxist literary critic who opposed the creation of a new proletarian culture but who insisted on the ideological content of literature.

4. Isaak Eventov, *Zhizn i tvorchestvo Demyana Bednogo* [*The Life and Works of Demyan Bedny*], p. 270.

5. Yevgeny Zamyatin, *Povesti i rasskazy* [*Tales and Stories*], pp. 246–47.

6. Mikhail Bulgakov, *Master i Margarita* [*The Master and Margarita*], p. 61.

7. Ilya Ilf and Yevgeny Petrov, *Sobranie sochineny v pyati tomakh* [*Collected Works in Five Volumes*], 4:23.

8. Ibid., 4:46.

9. Ibid., 4:198.

10. Ibid., 4:328.

11. Ibid., 4:355.

12. Ibid., 4:50.

13. Ibid., 3:80–81.

14. Ibid., 4:327.

15. Ibid., 4:419–20, 421.

16. Bulgakov, *The Master and Margarita*, p. 195.

17. M. V. Glenny, "Mikhail Bulgakov," *Survey* 65 (October 1967) :9.

Bibliography

Original Sources and English Translations

Averchenko, Arkady. *Chudesa v reshete: Rasskazy* [*Wonders Most Strange: Stories*]. Paris: Biblioteka "Illyustrirovannoy Rossii," 1935.
———. *Deti: Kniga novykh rasskasov* [*Children: A Book of New Stories*]. Constantinople: Kultura, 1922.
———. *Dyuzhina nozhey v spinu revolyutsii: 12 novykh rasskazov* [*A Dozen Knives in the Revolution's Back: Twelve New Stories*]. Paris: Bibliothèque Universelle, 1921.
———. *Dvenadtsat portretov* [*Twelve Portraits*]. Prague: Internationale Commerciale Revue, 1923.
———. *Izbrannoe* [*Selected Works*]. Washington, D.C.: Victor Kamkin, Inc., 1961.
———. *Nechistaya sila: Kniga novykh rasskazov* [*An Unclean Power: A Book of New Stories*]. Sevastopol: Novy Satirikon, 1920.
———. *Otdykh na krapive: Novaya kniga rasskazov* [*Relaxation in the Stinging Nettle: A New Book of Stories*]. Warsaw: Dobro, 1924.
———. *Podkhodtsev i dvoe drugikh* [*Podkhodtsev and Two Others*]. Paris: Biblioteka "Illyustrirovannoy Rossii," 1935.
———. *Rasskazy tsinika* [*Stories of a Cynic*]. Prague: Plamya, 1925.
———. *Ray na zemle: Pravdivye rasskazy o russkoy kommune* [*Paradise on Earth: True Stories of the Russian Commune*]. Zagreb: Khorvatsky Shtamparsky Zavod, 1922.
———. *Razvorochenny muraveynik: Emigrantskie rasskazy* [*The Toppled Anthill: Emigré Stories*]. Moscow: Zemlya i Fabrika, 1927.
———. *Yumoristicheskie rasskazy* [*Humorous Stories*]. Moscow: Khudozhestvennaya literatura, 1964.
Bedny, Demyan (pseudonym of Yefim Pridvorov). *Sobranie sochineny v vosmi tomakh* [*Collected Works in Eight Volumes*]. Moscow: Khudozhestvennaya literatura, 1965.
Buchinskaya, N. A. *See* Teffi, N. A.
Bulgakov, Mikhail. *Black Snow.* Translated by Michael Glenny. New York: Simon and Schuster, 1968.
———. *Diaboliad and Other Stories.* Translated by Carl Proffer. Bloomington: Indiana University Press, 1972.
———. *Dramy i komedii* [*Dramas and Comedies*]. Moscow: Iskusstvo, 1965.
———. *Dyavoliada: Rasskazy* [*Deviltry: Stories*]. Moscow: Nedra, 1925.
———. *The Early Plays of Mikhail Bulgakov.* Translated by Carl and Ellendea Proffer. Bloomington: Indiana University Press, 1972.
———. *Heart of a Dog.* Translated by Mirra Ginsburg. New York: Grove Press, 1968.
———. *Ivan Vasilievich: Myortvye dushi* [*Ivan Vasilievich: Dead Souls*]. Munich: Tovarishchestvo Zarubezhnykh Pisateley, 1964.
———. *Izbrannaya proza* [*Selected Prose*]. Moscow: Khudozhestvennaya literatura, 1966.

------. *The Master and Margarita*. Translated by Michael Glenny. New York: Harper and Row, 1967.

------. *Master i Margarita* [*The Master and Margarita*]. Paris: YMCA Press, 1968.

------. *Romany: Belaya gvardia, Teatralny roman, Master i Margarita* [*Novels: The White Guard, A Theatrical Novel, The Master and Margarita*]. Moscow: Khudozhestvennaya literatura, 1973.

------. *Sbornik rasskazov* [*A Collection of Stories*]. New York: Chekhov Publishing House, 1952.

------. *Sobachie serdtse* [*Heart of a Dog*]. Paris: YMCA Press, 1969.

------. *The White Guard*. Translated by Michael Glenny. New York: McGraw-Hill, 1971.

------. "Zoia's Apartment: A Play in Four Acts." Translated by Carl and Ellendea Proffer. *Canadian Slavic Studies* 4 (Summer 1970): 238–80.

------. "Zoykina kvartira" ["Zoya's Apartment"]. *Novy zhurnal* 97 (December 1969): 57–96; 98 (March 1970): 55–88.

Chyorny, A. (pseudonym of Alexander Glyukberg). *Satiry: Kniga pervaya* [*Satires: Book One*]. Berlin: Grani, 1922.

Don-Aminado (pseudonym of Aminad Shpolyansky). *Dym bez otechestva* [*Smoke without the Fatherland*]. Paris: Sever, 1921.

------. *Nakinuv plashch: Sbornik liricheskoy satiry* [*Putting on the Cloak: A Collection of Lyrical Satire*]. Paris: Neskuchny sad, 1928.

------. *Nasha malenkaya zhizn* [*Our Small Life*]. Paris: Ya. Povolotsky & Co., 1927.

Ehrenburg, Ilia. *The Extraordinary Adventures of Julio Jurenito and His Disciples*. Translated by U. Vanzler. New York: Covici-Friede, 1930.

------. *The Stormy Life of Laz Roitshvantz*. Translated by Alec Brown. London: Elek Books, 1965.

Ehrenburg, Ilya. *Fabrika snov: khronika nashego vremeni* [*The Dream Factory: A Chronicle of Our Time*]. Berlin: Petropolis, 1931.

------. *Memoires: 1921–1941*. Translated by Tatania Shebunina with Yvonne Kapp. Cleveland: World Publishing Company, 1964.

------. *Neobychaynye pokhozhdenia Khulio Khurenito i yego uchenikov: mosie Dele, Karla Shmidta, mistera Kulya, Alexeya Tishina, Erkole Bambuchi, Ili Erenburga, i negra Ayshi, v dni mira, voyny, i revolyutsii, v Parizhe, v Mexike, v Rime, v Senegale, v Kineshme, v Moskve i v drugikh mestakh, a takzhe razlichnye suzhdenia uchitelya o trubkakh, o smerti, o lyubvi, o svobode, ob igre v shakhmaty, o yevreyskom plemeni, o konstruktsii i o mnogom inom* [*The Extraordinary Adventures of Julio Jurenito and his Disciples: Monsieur Delais, Karl Schmidt, Mister Cool, Alexey Tishin, Ercole Bambucci, Ilya Ehrenburg, and the Negro Aysha, in Days of Peace, War, and Revolution, in Paris, Mexico, Rome, Senegal, Kineshma, Moscow, and Other Places, and Also Various Opinions of the Teacher About Pipes, Death, Love, Freedom, Chess, Jews, Construction, and Many Other Things*] (Moscow-Berlin: Gelikon, 1922).

------. *Sobranie sochineny v devyati tomakh* [*Collected Works in Nine Volumes*]. Moscow: Khudozhestvennaya literatura, 1962.

Erdman, Nikolai. *Two Plays: "The Mandate" and "The Suicide"*. Translated by Genereux, Volkov, and Hoover. Ann Arbor, Michigan: Ardis, 1975.

Fedin, Konstantin. *Narovchatskaya khronika* [*Narovchatskaya Chronicle*]. Vol. 6 of *Sochinenia v shesti tomakh* [*Works in Six Volumes*]. Moscow: Khudozhestvennaya literatura, 1954.

Ginsburg, Mirra, ed. and trans. *The Fatal Eggs and Other Satire*. New York: The Macmillan Company, 1965.

Gladkov, Fedor. *Cement*. Translated by A. S. Arthur and C. Ashleigh. New York: Frederick Ungar Publishing Company, 1960.

Gladkov, Fyodor. *Malenkaya trilogia* [*A Little Trilogy*]. Vol. 2 of *Sobranie sochineny v semi tomakh* [*Collected Works in Seven Volumes*]. Moscow: Khudozhestvennaya literatura, 1966.

———. *Tsement* [*Cement*]. Vol. 2, *Collected Works in Seven Volumes*. Moscow: Khudozhestvennaya literatura, 1966.

Glyukberg, Alexander. *See* Chyorny, A.

Gogol, Nikolay. *Dead Souls*. Translated by B. G. Guerney. New York: Modern Library, 1965.

———. *The Government Inspector*. Translated by Edward O. Marsh and Jeremy Brooks. London: Methuen, 1968.

———. *The Overcoat and Other Tales of Good and Evil*. Translated by David Magarshack. New York: Norton, 1965.

———. *Sobranie sochineny v semi tomakh* [*Collected Works in Seven Volumes*]. Moscow: Khudozhestvennaya literatura, 1966.

Gorky, Maxim. *Sobranie sochineny v tridtsati tomakh* [*Collected Works in Thirty Volumes*]. Moscow: Khudozhestvennaya literatura, 1949–55.

Henry, Peter. *Anthology of Soviet Satire*. Vols. 1, 2. London: Collet's Publishers Ltd., 1972, 1975.

Ilf, Ilia, and Petrov, Evgenii. *The Golden Calf*. Translated by John Richardson. New York: Random House, 1962.

———. *The Little Golden America: Two Famous Humorists Survey These United States*. Translated by John Richardson. New York: Farrar & Rinehart, 1937.

———. *The Twelve Chairs*. Translated by John Richardson. New York: Random House, 1937.

Ilf, Ilya, and Petrov, Yevgeny. *Sobranie sochineny v pyati tomakh* [*Collected Works in Five Volumes*]. Moscow: Khudozhestvennaya literatura, 1961.

Kataev, Valentin. *Borodaty malyutka: Yumoristicheskie rasskazy* [*The Bearded Baby: Humorous Stories*]. Riga: Gramatu draugs, 1929.

———. *Nozhi: Yumoristicheskie povesti i rasskazy* [*Knives: Humorous Tales and Stories*]. Moscow: Federatsia, 1930.

———. *Pesy* [*Plays*]. Moscow: Sovetsky pisatel, 1955.

———. *Sobranie sochineny v devyati tomakh* [*Collected Works in Nine Volumes*]. Moscow: Khudozhestvennaya literatura, 1969.

———. *Sobranie sochineny v pyati tomakh* [*Collected Works in Five Volumes*]. Moscow: Khudozhestvennaya literatura, 1956.

Katayev, Valentin. *The Embezzlers*. Translated by Leonide Zarine. London: Benn, 1929.

———. *Squaring the Circle*. Translated by N. Goold-Verschoyle. London: Wishart, 1934.

———. *Time, Forward!* Translated by Charles Malamuth. New York: Farrar & Rinehart, 1933.

Koltsov, Mikhail. *Izbrannye proizvedenia* [*Selected Works*]. Moscow: Khudozhestvennaya literatura, 1957.

Lebedev-Kumach, Vasily. *Lirika. Satira. Feleton* [*Lyrics. Satires. Feuilletons*]. Moscow: Iskusstvo, 1939.

———. *Lyudi i lyudishki* [*People and Little People*]. Moscow: Gudok, 1927.

Leonov, Leonid. *Zapisi nekotorykh epizodov, sdelannye v gorode Gogulyove Andreem Petrovichem Kovyakinym* [*Notes on Some Episodes Perpetrated in the City of Gogulyov by Andrey Petrovich Kovyakin*]. Vol. 1 of *Sobranie sochineny v devyati tomakh* [*Collected Works in Nine Volumes*]. Moscow: Khudozhestvennaya literatura, 1960.

Leskov, Nikolai. *Satirical Stories of Nikolai Leskov*. Translated by William B. Edgerton. New York: Western Publishing Company, 1969.

Leskov, Nikolay. *Sobranie sochineny v odinnadtsati tomakh* [*Collected Works in Eleven Volumes*]. Moscow: Khudozhestvennaya literatura, 1958.

Lyons, E., ed. *Six Soviet Plays*. New York: Houghton Mifflin, 1934.

MacAndrew, Andrew R., ed. and trans. *Twentieth Century Russian Drama*. New York: Bantam Books, 1963.

Marshak, Samuil. *Sochineny v chetyryokh tomakh* [*Works in Four Volumes*]. Moscow: Goslitizdat, 1958–60.

Marshall, Herbert, ed. and trans. *Mayakovsky*. New York: Hill and Wang, 1965.

Mayakovsky, Vladimir. *The Complete Plays*. Translated by G. Daniels. New York: Meridian Books, 1960.

——. *Satira* [*Satire*]. Moscow: Khudozhestvennaya literatura, 1953.

——. *Sobranie sochineny v vosmi tomakh* [*Collected Works in Eight Volumes*]. Moscow: Pravda, 1968.

Olesha, Yuri. *Envy and Other Works*. Translated by Andrew R. MacAndrew. Garden City, N.Y.: Anchor Books, 1967.

Olesha, Yurii. *Izbrannoe: Zavist' i drugie* [*Selected Works: Envy and Others*]. Pullman, Michigan: Russian Language Specialties, 1973.

Olesha, Yury. *Pesy* [*Plays*]. Moscow: Iskusstvo, 1968.

——. *Povesti i rasskazy* [*Tales and Stories*]. Moscow: Khudozhestvennaya literatura, 1965.

Pilnyak, Boris (pseudonym of Boris Vogau). *Goly god* [*The Naked Year*]. Letchworth, England: Bradda Books Ltd., 1966.

——. *Mother Earth and Other Stories*. Translated by Vera T. Rech and Michael Green. New York: Frederick A. Praeger, 1968.

——. *The Naked Year*. Translated by A. Brown. New York: Payson and Clark, 1928.

Platonov, Andrei. *Chevengur*. Translated by Anthony Olcott. Ann Arbor, Michigan: Ardis, 1978.

——. *Collected Works*. Ann Arbor, Michigan: Ardis, 1978.

Platonov, Andrey. *Izbrannoe* [*Selected Works*]. Moscow: Moskovsky rabochy, 1966.

Pridvorov, Yefim. *See* Bedny, Demyan.

Remizov, Alexey. *Pyataya yazva* [*The Fifth Pestilence*]. Berlin: Z. I. Grzhebin, 1922.

——. *V rozovom bleske* [*On a Field Azure*]. New York: Chekhov Publishing House, 1952.

——. *Vzvikhryonnaya Rus* [*Turbulent Russia*]. Paris: Tair, 1927.

Romanov, Panteleymon. *Yumoristicheskie rasskazy* [*Humorous Stories*]. Moscow: Ogonyok, 1926.

——. *Zemletryasenie* [*The Earthquake*]. Moscow: Teatralnoe izdatelstvo, 1924.

Romashov, Boris. *Pesy* [*Plays*]. Moscow: Sovetsky pisatel, 1954.

——. *Vmeste s vami* [*Together with You*]. Moscow: Vserossyskoe teatralnoe obshchestvo, 1964.

Saltykov, Mikhail. *Polnoe sobranie sochineny* [*Complete Collected Works*]. St. Petersburg: A. F. Marx, 1906.

Shishko, Anatoly. *Gospodin Antikhrist* [*Mr. Antichrist*]. Moscow: Zif, 1926.

——. *Komedia masok* [*A Comedy of Masks*]. Moscow: Zif, 1928.

——. *Konets zdravogo smysla* [*An End to Sanity*]. Moscow: Zif, 1927.

Shishkov, Vyacheslav. *Sobranie sochineny* [*Collected Works*]. Moscow: Pravda, 1974.

Shmelyov, Ivan. *Eto bylo: Rasskaz strannogo cheloveka* [*It Happened: The Story of a Strange Man*]. Berlin: Gamaium, 1923.

——. *Inexhaustible Cup*. Translated by Tatiana Dechtereva France. New York: E. P. Dutton, 1928.

——. *Neupivaemaya chasha i drugie rasskazy* [*The Inexhaustible Cup and Other Stories*]. Prague: Plamya, 1924.

——. *Pro odnu starukhu: Novye rasskazy o Rossii* [*About an Old Woman: New Stories about Russia*]. Paris: Tair, 1927.

——. *Solntse myortvykh* [*The Sun of the Dead*]. Paris: Vozrozhdenie-La Renaissance, 1949.

——. *The Sun of the Dead*. Translated by C. J. Hogarth. New York: E. P. Dutton, 1927.

Shpolyansky, Aminad. *See* Don-Aminado.

Sostschenko, M. *Wovon die Nachtigall Sang: O chyom pel solovey* [*What the Nightingale Sang*]. Frankfurt: Possev-Verlag, 1964.

Teffi, N. A. (pseudonym of N. A. Buchinskaya). *Chyorny iris: rasskazy* [*Black Iris: Stories*]. Stockholm: Severnye ogni, 1921.

———. *Kniga iyun* [*The June Book*]. Belgrade: Russkaya biblioteka, 1931.

———. *Nichego podobnogo* [*Nothing Like It*]. St. Petersburg: Novy Satirikon, n.d.

———. *Rys* [*At a Trot*]. Berlin: Otto Kirchner, 1923.

———. *Tak zhili* [*Thus They Lived*]. Stockholm: Severnye ogni, 1922.

———. *Vecherny den: Rasskazy* [*An Evening Day: Stories*]. Prague: Plamya, 1924.

———. *Yumoristicheskie rasskazy* [*Humorous Stories*]. St. Petersburg: Shipovnik, 1911.

Tolstoy, Alexey Nikolaevich. *The Death Box.* Translated by B. G. Guerney. London: Methuen, 1936.

———. *Polnoe sobranie sochineny* [*Complete Collected Works*]. Moscow: Khudozhestvennaya literatura, 1948.

Tretiakov, Sergei. *Roar, China!* Translated by E. Polianovska and B. Nixon. London: Lawrence, 1931.

Volkov, Mikhail. *Sobranie sochineny* [*Collected Works*]. Moscow: Moskovskoe tovarishchestvo pisateley, 1928.

Zamyatin, Eugene. *We.* Translated by G. Zilboorg. New York: Dutton, 1959.

Zamyatin, Yevgeny. "Afrikansky gost: Neveroyatnoe proisshestvie v 3-kh chasakh" ["The African Guest: An Improbable Occurrence in Three Hours"]. *Novy zhurnal* 73 (September 1963): 38–96.

———. *The Dragon: Fifteen Stories.* Translated and edited by Mirra Ginsburg. New York: Random House, 1967.

———. *Litsa* [*Faces*]. New York: Chekhov Publishing House, 1955.

———. "Mucheniki nauki" ["Martyrs of Science"]. *Novy zhurnal* 72 (March 1963): pp. 12–36.

———. *My* [*We*]. New York: Chekhov Publishing House, 1952.

———. *Povesti i rasskazy* [*Tales and Stories*]. Munich: Tsentralnoe obedinenie politicheskikh emigrantov iz SSSR, 1963.

———. *Sobranie sochineny* [*Collected Works*]. 4 vols. Moscow: Federatsia, 1929.

Zoshchenko, Mikhail. *Izbrannoe* [*Selected Stories*]. Ann Arbor: University of Michigan Press, 1960.

———. *Izbrannye proizvedenia v dvukh tomakh* [*Selected Works in Two Volumes*]. Leningrad: Khudozhestvennaya literatura, 1968.

———. *Nad kem smeyotes* [*Who Are You Laughing At?*]. Riga: Mif, 1928.

———. *Nervnye lyudi* [*Nervous People*]. Riga: Mif, 1928.

———. *Nervous People and Other Satires.* Edited by Hugh McLean. London: Victor Gollancz Ltd., 1963.

———. *O tom, chto bylo i chego ne bylo: Novye rasskazy* [*About That Which Was and Was Not: New Stories*]. Riga: Literatura, 1928.

———. *Povesti i rasskazy* [*Tales and Stories*]. Leningrad: Sovetsky pisatel, 1959.

———. *Priyatnaya vstrecha: Novye povesti i rasskazy* [*A Pleasant Meeting: New Tales and Stories*]. Riga: Knizhnaya lavka pisateley, 1930.

———. *Rasskazy* [*Stories*]. Moscow: Khudozhestvennaya literatura, 1974.

———. *Russia Laughs.* Translated by H. Clayton. Boston: Lothrop, Lee & Shepard, 1935.

———. *Scenes from the Bathhouse and Other Stories of Communist Russia.* Ann Arbor: University of Michigan Press, 1961.

———. *Semeyny kuporos* [*Family Feud*]. Berlin: Petropolis, 1929.

———. *Skupoy rytsar: Rasskazy* [*The Covetous Knight: Stories*]. Riga: Literatura, 1928.

———. *Sobranie sochineny* [*Collected Works*]. Leningrad: Khudozhestvennaya literatura, 1929–31.

———. *Vesyoloe priklyuchenie* [*A Merry Adventure*]. Berlin: Petropolis, 1927.

——. *The Woman Who Could Not Read and Other Stories*. Translated by Elisaveta Fen. London: Methuen, 1940.
——. *The Wonderful Dog and Other Tales*. Translated by Elisaveta Fen. London: Methuen, 1942.

SELECTED CRITICAL WORKS AND BACKGROUND READING

Alexandrova, Vera. *A History of Soviet Literature*. Translated by Mirra Ginsburg. Garden City, N.Y.: Doubleday, 1963.

Ansberg, Aleksei. "Frame Story and First Person Story in N. S. Leskov." *Scando-Slavica* 3 (1957):49–74.

Barghoorn, Frederick. *The Soviet Image of the United States: A Study in Distortion*. New York: Harcourt, Brace, 1950.

Begak, Boris. *Russkaya literaturnaya parodia* [*Russian Literary Parody*]. Moscow: Gosudarstvennoe izdatelstvo, 1930.

Benjamin, Walter. "The Story-Teller: Reflections on the Works of Nicolai Leskov." Translated by Harry Zohn. *Chicago Review* 16 (Winter-Spring 1963):80–123.

Borland, Harriet. *Soviet Literary Theory and Practice during the First Five-Year Plan 1928–1932*. New York: King's Crown Press, 1950.

Bristol, Evelyn. "Boris Pil'nyak." *Slavonic and East European Review* 41 (June 1963):494–512.

Bronshteyn, Lev. See Trotsky, Leon.

Brown, Deming. *Soviet Attitudes toward American Writing*. Princeton: Princeton University Press, 1962.

Brown, Edward J. *The Proletarian Episode in Russian Literature 1928–1932*. New York: Columbia University Press, 1953.

——. *Russian Literature since the Revolution*. New York: Collier Books, 1963.

——. "Zamiatin and English Literature." *American Contributions to the Fifth International Congress of Slavicists* 2 (1963):21–40.

Bushmin, A. S. *Satira Saltykova-Shchedrina* [*The Satire of Saltykov-Shchedrin*]. Leningrad: AN SSSR, 1959.

Carter, Huntley. *The New Spirit in the Russian Theatre 1917–1928*. London: Brentano's Ltd., 1929.

Chukovsky, Korney. "Mikhail Zoshchenko: Iz vospominany" ["Mikhail Zoshchenko: From Memoires"]. *Moskva* 9 (June 1965):190–208.

Collins, Christopher. *Evgenij Zamjatin: An Interpretive Study*. The Hague: Mouton, 1973.

——. "Zamiatin's We as Myth." *The Slavic and East European Journal* 10 (Spring 1966):125–34.

Ducharte, Pierre Louis. *The Italian Comedy*. Translated by Randolph T. Weaver. New York: Dover Publications, Inc., 1966.

Dzhivelegov, A. K. *Italyanskaya narodnaya komedia* [*Italian Folk Comedy*]. Moscow: AN SSSR, 1962.

Eastman, Max. *Artist in Uniform: A Study of Literature and Bureaucracy*. New York: Alfred A. Knopf, 1934.

Edgerton, William B. "The Serapion Brothers: An Early Soviet Controversy." *The American Slavic and East European Review* 8 (February 1949):47–64.

Elliott, Robert C. *The Power of Satire: Magic, Ritual, Art*. Princeton: Princeton University Press, 1960.

Elsberg, Yakov. *Nasledie Gogolya i Shchedrina i sovetskaya satira* [*Soviet Satire and the Legacy of Gogol and Shchedrin*]. Moscow: Sovetsky pisatel, 1954.

——. *Voprosy teorii satiry* [*Questions on the Theory of Satire*]. Moscow: Sovetsky pisatel, 1957.

Eng-Liedmeier, A. M. van der. *Soviet Literary Characters: An Investigation into the Portrayal of Soviet Men in Russian Prose 1917–1953.* The Hague: Mouton, 1959.

Erlich, Victor. "The Dead Hand of the Future: The Predicament of Vladimir Mayakovsky." *Slavic Review* 21 (September 1962):433–41.

————. *The Double Image: Concepts of the Poet in Slavic Literatures.* Baltimore: Johns Hopkins University Press, 1964.

————. *Gogol.* New Haven: Yale University Press, 1969.

————. "A Note on the Grotesque. Gogol: A Test Case." *Janua Linguarum* 31 (October 1966):630–34.

————. *Russian Formalism: History–Doctrine.* The Hague: Mouton, 1955.

Ermolaev, Herman. *Soviet Literary Theories 1917–1934: The Genesis of Socialist Realism.* Berkeley: University of California Press, 1963.

Eventov, Isaak. *Satira v tvorchestve M. Gorkogo [Satire in the Works of Maxim Gorky].* Leningrad: Sovetsky pisatel, 1962.

————. *Zhizn i tvorchestvo Demyana Bednogo [The Life and Works of Demyan Bedny].* Leningrad: Khudozhestvennaya literatura, 1967.

Feinberg, Leonard. *The Satirist: His Temperament, Motivation, and Influence.* Ames: Iowa State University Press, 1963.

Foster, Liudmila A. *Bibliography of Russian Emigré Literature, 1918–1968.* Boston: G. K. Hall & Co., 1968.

Friedberg, Maurice. "A Note on Soviet Satire." *Survey* 4 (April-June 1961):110–14.

————. *Russian Classics in Soviet Jackets.* New York: Columbia University Press, 1962.

Gasiorowska, Xenia. *Women in Soviet Fiction 1917–1964.* Madison: University of Wisconsin Press, 1968.

Gifford, Henry. *The Novel in Russia: From Pushkin to Pasternak.* London: Hutchinson, 1964.

Goryachkina, Maria. *Satira Saltykova-Shchedrina [The Satire of Saltykov-Shchedrin].* Moscow: Prosveshchenie, 1965.

Gul, Roman. "A. Solzhenitsyn, sotsrealizm i shkola Remizova" ["A. Solzhenitsyn, Socialist Realism and the Remizov School"]. *Novy zhurnal* 72 (March 1963): 58–75.

Gulbinsky, Ignaty. *Literatura velikogo desyatiletia, 1917–1927 [The Literature of the Great Decade, 1917–1927].* Moscow: Gosudarstvennoe izdatelstvo, 1928.

Hare, Richard. *Maxim Gorky: Romantic Realist and Conservative Revolutionary.* New York: Oxford University Press. 1962.

Hayward, Max, and Labedz, Leopold, eds. *Literature and Revolution in Soviet Russia 1917–1962.* New York: Oxford University Press, 1963.

Hrala, Milan. "O vztahu tragického a komického prvku u Michaila Zoščenka" ["The Relationship of the Tragic and Comic in the Works of Mikhail Zoshchenko"]. *Československá rusistika* 11 (April 1966):34–39.

Institut russkoy literatury [Institute of Russian Literature]. *Voprosy sovetskoy literatury [Questions of Soviet Literature].* Vol. 5. Leningrad: AN SSSR, 1957.

Kayser, Wolfgang. *The Grotesque in Art and Literature.* Translated by Ulrich Weisstein. New York: McGraw-Hill, 1966.

Kernan, Alvin B. *The Plot of Satire.* New Haven: Yale University Press, 1965.

Kiparsky, Valentin. *English and American Characters in Russian Fiction.* Veröffentlichungen der Abteilung für Slavische Sprachen und Literaturen des Osteuropa-Instituts (Slavisches Seminar). Vol. 31. Berlin: die Freie Universität Berlin, 1964.

Kodryanskaya, Natalia. *Alexey Remizov.* Paris, 1959.

Kratkaya literaturnaya entsiklopedia [The Short Literary Encyclopedia]. Moscow: Sovetskaya entsiklopedia, 1962–75.

Krejči, Karel. "Satira a groteska" ["Satire and the Grotesque"]. *Československá rusistika* 11 (April 1966):1–6.

Leyburn, Ellen Douglas. *Satiric Allegory: Mirror of Man.* New York: Yale University Press, 1956.

Lo Gatto, Ettore. *La letteratura russo-sovietica* [*Soviet Russian Literature*]. Florence: Sansoni, 1968.

———. *La letteratura sovietica* [*Soviet Literature*]. Rome, 1929.

———. *Storia del teatro russo* [*History of the Russian Theater*]. 2 vols. Florence: Sansoni, 1952.

McLean, Hugh. "On the Style of the Leskovian Skaz." *Harvard Slavic Studies* 2 (1954): 297–322.

Maguire, Robert A. *Red Virgin Soil: Soviet Literature in the 1920's.* Princeton: Princeton University Press, 1968.

Mandelshtam, Yury. *O kharaktere gogolevskogo stilya* [*On the Characteristics of Gogol's Style*]. St. Petersburg: Gelsingfors, 1902.

Markiewicz, Henry. "On the Definition of Literary Parody." *Janua Linguarum* 31 (October 1966):1264–73.

Markov, P. A. *The Soviet Theater.* London: Victor Gollancz, Ltd., 1934.

Markov, Vladimir. *Russian Futurism: A History.* Berkeley: University of California Press, 1968.

Mashbits-Verov, I. *Poemy Mayakovskogo* [*Mayakovsky's Poems*]. Moscow: Sovetsky pisatel, 1963.

Mathauserova, Světla. "Barokní groteska a klasicistní satira" ["Baroque Grotesque and Classical Satire"]. *Československá rusistika* 11 (April 1966):9–14.

Mikulášek, Miroslav. "Nekotorye voprosy sovetskoy satiricheskoy komedii i tvorchesky put Mayakovskogo" ["Some Questions about the Soviet Satirical Comedy and the Creative Path of Mayakovsky"]. *Československá rusistika* 11 (April 1966):28–34.

Milyavsky, B. *Satirik i vremya: O masterstve Mayakovskogo-dramaturga* [*The Satirist and Time: Mayakovsky's Mastery as a Dramatist*]. Moscow: Sovetsky pisatel, 1963.

Mirsky, D. S. *Contemporary Russian Literature: 1881–1925.* New York: Alfred A. Knopf, 1926.

Moser, Charles A. "Mayakovsky's Unsentimental Journeys." *The American Slavic and East European Review* 14 (February 1960):85–101.

Muchnic, Helen. *From Gorky to Pasternak: Six Writers in Soviet Russia.* New York: Random House, 1961.

Naumov, E. I. *Seminary po Mayakovskomu* [*A Mayakovsky Seminar*]. Leningrad: Gosudarstvennoe uchebno-pedagogicheskoe izdatelstvo Ministerstva prosveshchenia RSFSR, 1955.

Nilsson, Nils Åke. "Through the Wrong End of Binoculars: An Introduction to Jurij Oleša." *Scando-Slavica* 11 (1965):40–69.

O'Connor, William Van. *The Grotesque: An American Genre and Other Essays.* Carbondale: Southern Illinois University Press, 1962.

Oulanoff, Hongor. "Motives of Pessimism in Erenburg's Early Works." *The Slavic and East European Journal* 11 (Fall 1967):266–78.

———. *The Serapion Brothers: Theory and Practice.* The Hague: Mouton, 1966.

Ozmitel, E. K. *Sovetskaya satira: Seminary* [*A Seminar on Soviet Satire*]. Moscow: Prosveshchenie, 1964.

Paulson, Ronald. *The Fictions of Satire.* Baltimore: The Johns Hopkins University Press, 1967.

Perlman, Louis. *Russian Literature and the Businessman.* New York: Columbia University Press, 1967.

Poggioli, Renato. *The Phoenix and the Spider.* Cambridge: Harvard University Press, 1957.

———. *The Poets of Russia 1890–1930.* Cambridge: Harvard University Press, 1960.

Poplyuyko, A. "Khirurgia *Khulio Khurenito*" ["The Surgery on *Julio Jurenito*"]. *Grani* 20 (January 1965):158–64.

Proffer, Carl. "Notes on the Imagery in Zamjatin's *We.*" *The Slavic and East European Journal* 7 (Fall 1963):158–64.

Reavy, George. *Soviet Literature Today*. New Haven: Yale University Press, 1947.

Reeve, F. D. "A Geometry of Prose." *The Kenyon Review* 25 (Winter 1963):9–25.

Rev, Maria. "Obraz Iudushki i nekotorye voprosy satiricheskogo i psikhologicheskogo izobrazhenia" ["The Image of Iudushka and Some Questions on Satirical and Psychological Depiction"]. *Studia Slavica* 13 (1967):47–88.

Richards, D. J. *Zamyatin: A Soviet Heretic*. New York: Hillary House Publishers Ltd., 1962.

Ruzhina, V. *Mayakovsky protiv religii [Mayakovsky against Religion]*. Kishinyov: Kartia moldoveniaskè, 1967.

Sayler, O. M. *Russian Theatre under the Revolution*. New York: Brentano's Ltd., 1922.

Schulz, Robert Kenneth. *The Portrayal of the German in Russian Novels: Gončarov, Turgenev, Dostoevskij, Tolstoj*. Slavistische Beiträge Band 42. Munich: Verlag Otto Sagner, 1969.

Sedgewick, G. G. *Of Irony, Especially in the Drama*. University of Toronto Studies, vol. 10. Toronto: University of Toronto Press, 1968.

Shane, Alex M. *The Life and Works of Evgenii Zamjatin*. Berkeley: University of California Press, 1968.

———. "Zamjatin's Prose Fiction." *The Slavic and East European Journal* 12 (Spring 1968):14–26.

Sharpe, Robert Boies. *Irony in the Drama: An Essay on Impersonation, Shock, and Catharsis*. Chapel Hill: University of North Carolina Press, 1959.

Sidelnikova, T. *Valentin Kataev: Ocherk zhizni i tvorchestva [Valentin Kataev: A Sketch of His Life and Works]*. Moscow: Sovetsky pisatel, 1957.

Simmons, Ernest J. *Russian Fiction and Soviet Ideology: Introduction to Fedin, Leonov, and Sholokhov*. New York: Columbia University Press, 1958.

———. ed. *Through the Glass of Soviet Literature: Views of Russian Society*. New York: Columbia University Press, 1964.

Slonim, Marc. *Russian Theatre: From the Empire to the Soviets*. New York: Collier, 1962.

———. *Soviet Russian Literature: Writers and Problems*. New York: Oxford University Press, 1964.

Smith, Winifred. *The Commedia Dell'Arte*. New York: Benjamin Blom, Inc., 1964.

Sorokin, Olga Gromov. "Ivan Šmelëv: His Life and Work." Ph.D. dissertation, University of California, Berkeley, 1965.

Starkov, A. N. "Ot Sinebryukhova k *Goluboy knige* (Satira M. Zoshchenko v 20-kh—pervoy polovine 30-kh godov: evolyutsia skaza") [From Sinebryukhov to *The Blue Book* (Mikhail Zoshchenko's Satire in the 1920's and First Half of the 1930's: The Evolution of the Skaz)]. *Voprosy literatury* 11 (November 1964):64–83.

———. *Voprosy teorii sovetskogo satiricheskogo feletona v kritike dvadtsatykh godov [Questions of the Theory of the Soviet Satirical Feuilleton in the Criticism of the 1920's]*. Izvestia akademii nauk SSSR, vol. 22, no. 6 (Moscow: AN SSSR), 1963.

Stone, Christopher. *Parody*. New York: George H. Doran Company, 1914.

Struve, Gleb. *Russian Literature under Lenin and Stalin 1917–1953*. Norman: University of Oklahoma Press, 1971.

———. *Russkaya literatura v izgnanii [Russian Literature in Exile]*. New York: Chekhov Publishing House, 1956.

———. *Soviet Russian Literature 1917–1950*. Norman: University of Oklahoma Press, 1951.

Stykelin, S., and Kremenskaya, I. *Sovetskaya satiricheskaya pechat 1917–1963 [The Soviet Satirical Press 1917–1963]*. Moscow: Politicheskaya literatura, 1963.

Thompson, Alan Reynolds, *The Dry Mock: A Study of Irony in the Drama*. Berkeley: University of California Press, 1948.

Trotsky, Leon (pseudonym of Lev Bronshteyn). *Literature and Revolution*. Translated by Rose Strunsky. New York: International Publishers, 1925.

Veksler, N. N. *Alexey Nikolaevich Tolstoy*. Moscow: Sovetsky pisatel, 1948.

Vickery, Walter. *The Cult of Optimism: Political and Ideological Problems of Recent Soviet Literature*. Bloomington: Indiana University Press, 1967.

Vinogradov, Viktor. *Etyudy o stile Gogolya [Studies in Gogol's Style]*. Leningrad: Academia, 1926.

Vogau, Boris. *See* Pilnyak, Boris.

Vulis, A. I. *Ilf, Ye. Petrov: Ocherk tvorchestva [I. Ilf and Ye. Petrov: A Sketch of Their Works]*. Moscow: Khudozhestvennaya literatura, 1960.

Vulliamy, C. E. *The Anatomy of Satire*. London: Michael Joseph, 1950.

Weil, Irwin. *Gorky: His Literary Development and Influence on Soviet Intellectual Life*. New York: Random House, 1966.

Wiren-Garczynski, Vera von. "Zoshchenko's Psychological Interests." *The Slavic and East European Journal* 11 (Spring, 1967):3–23.

Yarmolinsky, Avrahm. *Literature under Communism*. Bloomington: Indiana University Press, 1953.

Yefimov, Alexander. *Yazyk satiry Saltykova-Shchedrina [Saltykov-Shchedrin's Satirical Language]*. Moscow: Moskovsky universitet, 1953.

Yershov, L. F. *Sovetskaya satiricheskaya proza [Soviet Satirical Prose]*. Moscow: Khudozhestvennaya literatura, 1966.

―――. *Sovetskaya satiricheskaya proza 20-kh godov [Soviet Satirical Prose of the 1920's]*. Moscow: AN SSSR, 1960.

Yershov, P. *Comedy in the Soviet Theatre*. New York: Frederick A. Praeger Publishers, 1956.

Yevstigneeva, L. A. *Russkaya satira v gody mezhdu dvumya revolyutsiyami (1907–1917gg.) [Russian Satire in the Years between the Two Revolutions 1907–1917]*. Izvestia AN SSSR, vol 22. Moscow: AN SSSR; Otdelenie literatury i yazyka, 1963.

Zamyatin, Yevgeny. *A Soviet Heretic: Essays by Yevgeny Zamyatin*. Translated and edited by Mirra Ginsburg. Chicago: University of Chicago Press, 1970.

Zavalishin, Vyacheslav. *Early Soviet Writers*. New York: Frederick A. Praeger Publishers, 1958.

ADDITIONAL BIBLIOGRAPHY

Eventov, Isaak. *Sila sarkazma; Satira i yumor v tvorchestve M. Gorkogo [The Force of Sarcasm; Satire and Humor in the Work of M. Gorky]*. Leningrad: Sovetsky pisatel, 1973.

Institut russkoy literatury [Institute of Russian Literature]. *Russkaya sovetskaya povest 20–30kh godov [The Russian Soviet Tale in the 1920s and 1930s]*. Leningrad: Nauka, 1976.

Simkin, Ya. P. *Satiricheskaya publitsistika [Satirical Publicistic Work]*. Rostov: Izdatelstvo Rostovskogo universiteta, 1976.

Yershov, Leonid. *Iz istorii sovetskoy satiry; M. Zoshchenko i satiricheskaya proza 20–40kh godov [From the History of Soviet Satire; M. Zoshchenko and Satirical Prose of the 1920s–1940s]*. Leningrad: Nauka, 1973.

―――. *Satira i sovremennost [Satire and the Contemporary]*. Moscow: Sovremennik, 1978.

―――. *Satiricheskie zhanry russkoy sovetskoy literatury (Ot epigrammy do romana) [Satirical Genres in Russian Literature (From the Epigram to the Novel)]*. Leningrad: Nauka, 1977.

Index

UNIVERSITY OF FLORIDA MONOGRAPHS

Humanities

No. 1: *Uncollected Letters of James Gates Percival*, edited by Harry R. Warfel

No. 2: *Leigh Hunt's Autobiography: The Earliest Sketches*, edited by Stephen F. Fogle

No. 3: *Pause Patterns in Elizabethan and Jacobean Drama*, by Ants Oras

No. 4: *Rhetoric and American Poetry of the Early National Period*, by Gordon E. Bigelow

No. 5: *The Background of* The Princess Casamassima, by W. H. Tilley

No. 6: *Indian Sculpture in the John and Mable Ringling Museum of Art*, by Roy C. Craven, Jr.

No. 7: *The Cestus. A Mask*, edited by Thomas B. Stroup

No. 8: Tamburlaine, Part I, *and Its Audience*, by Frank B. Fieler

No. 9: *The Case of John Darrell: Minister and Exorcist*, by Corinne Holt Rickert

No. 10: *Reflections of the Civil War in Southern Humor*, by Wade H. Hall

No. 11: *Charles Dodgson, Semeiotician*, by Daniel F. Kirk

No. 12: *Three Middle English Religious Poems*, edited by R. H. Bowers

No. 13: *The Existentialism of Miguel de Unamuno*, by José Huertas-Jourda

No. 14: *Four Spiritual Crises in Mid-Century American Fiction*, by Robert Detweiler

No. 15: *Style and Society in German Literary Expressionism*, by Egbert Krispyn

No. 16: *The Reach of Art: A Study in the Prosody of Pope*, by Jacob H. Adler

No. 17: *Malraux, Sartre, and Aragon as Political Novelists*, by Catherine Savage

No. 18: *Las Guerras Carlistas y el Reinado Isabelino en la Obra de Ramón del Valle-Inclán*, por María Dolores Lado

No. 19: *Diderot's* Vie de Sénèque: *A Swan Song Revised*, by Douglas A. Bonneville

No. 20: *Blank Verse and Chronology in Milton*, by Ants Oras

No. 21: *Milton's Elisions*, by Robert O. Evans

No. 22: *Prayer in Sixteenth-Century England*, by Faye L. Kelly

No. 23: *The Strangers: The Tragic World of Tristan L'Hermite*, by Claude K. Abraham

No. 24: *Dramatic Uses of Biblical Allusion in Marlowe and Shakespeare*, by James H. Sims

No. 25: *Doubt and Dogma in Maria Edgeworth*, by Mark D. Hawthorne